ISBN 0-933546-55-6

9 780933 546554 >

KHANIQAHI NIMATULLAHI
(CENTERS OF THE NIMATULLAHI SUFI ORDER)

306 West 11th Street
New York, New York 10014
Tel: 212-924-7739
Fax: 212-924-5479

4021 19th Avenue
San Francisco,
California 94132
Tel: 415-586-1313

4931 MacArthur Blvd. NW
Washington D.C. 20007
Tel: 202-338-4757

84 Pembroke Street
Boston Massachusetts 02118
Tel: 617-536-0076

310 NE 57th Street
Seattle, Washington 98105
Tel: 206-527-5018

11019 Arleta Avenue
Mission Hills,Los Angeles,
California 91345
Tel: 818-365-2226

4642 North Hermitage
Chicago, Illinois 60640
Tel:312-561-1616

405 Greg Avenue
Santa Fe, New Mexico 87501
Tel: 505-983-8500

219 Chace Street
Santa Cruz,
California 95060
Tel: 408-425-8454

95 Old Lansdowne Road
West Didsbury,
Manchester
M20 8NZ, United Kingdom
Tel: 061-434-8857

Kölnerstrasse 176
5000 Köln 90 (Porz)
Federal Republic of Germany
Tel: 49-2203-15390

50 Rue du 4eme Zouaves
Rosny-sous-Bois
Paris, 93110 France
Tel: 48552809

63 Boulevard Latrille
BP 1224 Abidjan
CIDEX 1 Côte d'Ivoire, Africa
Tel: 225-410510

87A Mullens Street
Balmain, Sydney,
Australia 2041
Tel: 612-555-7546

C/Abedul 11
Madrid 28036
Spain
Tel:341-350502086

41 Chepstow Place
London W2 4TS
United Kingdom
Tel: 071-229-0769
Fax: 071-221-7025

SUFI SYMBOLISM

Volume IX

Also available by Dr. Javad Nurbakhsh:

1. In the Tavern of Ruin: Seven Essays on Sufism
2. In the Paradise of the Sufis
3. What the Sufis Say
4. Masters of the Path
5. Divani Nurbakhsh: Sufi Poetry
6. Sufism (I): Meaning, Knowledge and Unity
7. Traditions of the Prophet, Vol. I
8. Sufism (II): Fear and Hope, Contraction and Expansion, Gathering and Dispersion, Intoxication and Sobriety, Annihilation and Subsistence
9. The Truths of Love: Sufi Poetry
10. Sufi Women
11. Traditions of the Prophet, Vol. II
12. Jesus in the Eyes of the Sufis
13. Spiritual Poverty in Sufism
14. Sufism III: Submission, Contentment, Absence, Presence, Intimacy, Awe, Tranquillity, Serenity, Fluctuation, Stability
15. Sufi Symbolism I: Parts of the Beloved's Body, Wine, Music, Sama and Convivial Gatherings
16. The Great Satan, 'Eblis'
17. Sufi Symbolism II: Love, Lover, Beloved,
18. Sufism IV: Repentance, Abstinence, Renunciation, Wariness, Humility, Humbleness, Sincerity, Constancy, Courtesy
19. Sufi Symbolism III: Religious Terminology
20. Dogs from the Sufi Point of View
21. Sufi Symbolism IV: The Natural World
22. Sufi Women: Revised Edition
23. Sufi Symbolism V: Veils and Clothing, Government, Economics and Commerce, Medicine and Healing
24. Psychology of Sufism (Del wa Nafs)
25. Sufi Symbolism VI: Titles and Epithets
26. Sufi Symbolism VII: Contemplative Disciplines, Visions and Theophanies, Family Relationships, Servants of God, Names of Sufi Orders
27. Sufi Symbolism VIII: Inspirations, Revelations, Lights, Charismatic Powers, Spiritual States and Stations, Praise and Condemnation

SUFI SYMBOLISM

THE NURBAKHSH ENCYCLOPDIA OF SUFI TERMINOLOGY
(FARHANG-E NURBAKHSH)

Volume IX

Spiritual Faculties,
Spiritual Organs,
Knowledge,
Gnosis,
Wisdom and
Perfection

By
Dr. Javad Nurbakhsh

KHANIQAHI-NIMATULLAHI PUBLICATIONS
LONDON NEW YORK

Translated by Terry Graham under the supervision of
Dr. Javad Nurbakhsh in collaboration with
Neal and Sima Johnston.
Designed by Jane Lewisohn

Printed in the United Kingdom
on acid free paper.

British Library Cataloging in publication data

Sufi Symbolism Volume IX

I. Javad Nurbakhsh
297.4

Hardback: ISBN
0-933546-55-6

First British Edition published 1995 by KNP
41 Chepstow Place
London W2 4TS
England
Tel:: 071-229-0769
Fax: 071-221-7025

CONTENTS

PART III: Knowledge, Gnosis, Wisdom and Perfection 115

ABBREVIATIONS

AN	*Asrār-nāma*
AT	*Asrār at-tauḥid*
D	*Farhang-e Dehkhodā*
EA	*Moḥye'd-Din ebn 'Arabi* (Dr. Jahāngiri)
EE	*Estelāḥāt-e 'Erāqi*
EKJ	*Ensan al-kāmel*
ES	*Eṣṭelāḥāt aṣ-ṣufiya*
FLM	*Farhang-e loqāt-e Mathnawi*
FM	*Fotuḥat al-makkiya*
HAu	*Haft Aurang*
HH	*Ḥadiqat al-ḥaqiqat wa shari'at aṭ-ṭariqat*
HY	*Ḥaqq al-yaqin*
JAZ	*jawāher al-asrār wa ẓawāher al-anwār*
KAM	*Kashf al-asrār* (Maibodi)
KF	*Kashshāf eṣṭelāḥāt al-fonun*
KM	*Kashf al-maḥjub*
KMf-	*Kanz al mad'fun*
KMk	*Kalamāt maknuna* (Fayḍh Kāshāni)
KS	*Kimiā-ye s'ādat*
KST	*Kholāṣa-ye sharḥ ta'arrof*
L	*Lawā'eḥ*
LG	*Laṭifa-ye ghaybi.*
Lm	*Resāla-ye lama'āt*

LT	*Loma' fe't-taṣawwof (Ketāb al-)*
M	*Mathnawihā-ye Sanā'i*
MA	*Mashrab al-arwāḥ*
MAM	*Marmuzāt al-asadi*
MAr	*Menāqeb al- 'ārefin*
ME	*Merṣād al-'ebād*
MH	*Meṣbāḥ al-hedāya wa meftāḥ al-kefāya.*
MjS	*Mo'jam aṣ-ṣufi*
MM	*Mathnawi-ye ma'nawi*
MN	*Moṣibat-nāma*
MqS	*Maqalāt-e Shams*
MS	*Manāzel as-sā'erin*
MT	*Manṭeq aṭ-ṭayr*
NF	*Nafā'es al-fonun*
NK	*Noṣuṣ al-khoṣuṣ*
NN	*Naqd an-nuṣuṣ*
NP	*Nān-o panir*
NsN	*Nosus al khusus*
RA	*Rashf al-alḥāẓ*
RAs	*Majmu'a-ye Rasā'el-e Khwāja 'Abdo'llāh-e Anṣāri*
RAj	*Rasā'el-e jāme'-e Khwāja 'Abdo'llāh-e Anṣāri*
RQ	*Tarjoma-ye resāla-ye Qoshairi.*
RQR	*Resālat al-qods* (Ruzbehān)
RSh	*Resālahā-ye Shāh Ne'mato'llāh-e Wali*
SGR	*Sharḥ-e Golshan-e rāz*
SM	*Ṣad maidān*
SMz	*Sharḥ manḍhuma-ye Ḥikmat*
SS	*Sharḥ-e shaṭḥiyāt*
TA	*Tadhkerat al-auliā'*
TJ	*Ta'rifāt-e Jorjāni*
TKQ	*Tarjoma-ye kalamāt-e qeṣār-e Bābā Ṭāhir*
TSA	*Ṭabaqāt aṣ-ṣufiya* (Anṣāri)
TSS	*Ṭabaqāt aṣ-ṣufiya* (Solami)
TT	*Taṣawwof wa adabiyāt-e taṣawwof* (including *Mer'āt-e 'oshshāq)*
Z	*Zād al-'ārefin*

TRANSLITERATION EQUIVALENTS

Consonants

Arabic	Latin	Arabic	Latin
ء	’	ض	ḍh (z)
ب	b	ط	ṭ
ت	t	ظ	ẓ
ث	th (s)*	ع	‘
ج	j	غ	gh
ح	ḥ	ف	f
خ	kh	ق	q
د	d	ك	k
ذ	dh (z)	ل	l
ر	r	م	m
ز	z	ن	n
س	s	و	w (v)
ش	sh	ه	h
ص	ṣ	ی	y
		ة	h

Long Vowels

Arabic	Latin
آ	ā
أو	u
ای	i

Short Vowels

Arabic	Latin
اَ	a
اُ	o
اِ	e

Diphthongs

Arabic	Latin
اَو	au
اَی	ai

Persian Consonants

Arabic	Latin	Arabic	Latin
پ	p	ژ	zh
چ	ch	گ	g

* Letters in parentheses indicate where Persian pronunciation of Arabic letters differs from the Arabic pronunciation.

Spiritual Faculties

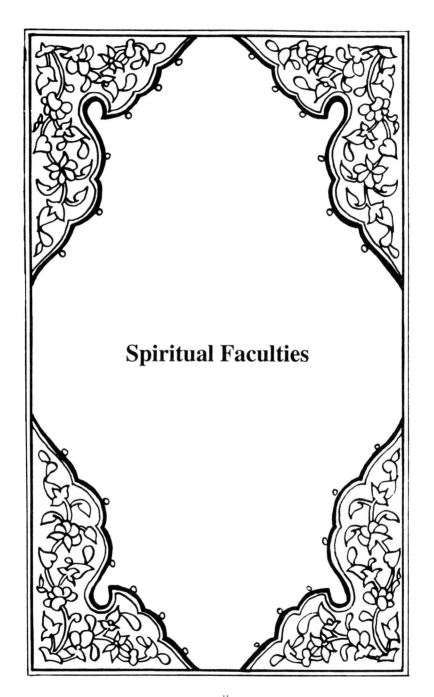

UNDERSTANDING *(sho'ur)*

In Sufi terminology, understanding is the first stage of the self's comprehension of meaning. When the self acquires awareness in the fullest sense, this is known as conceptualization *(taṣawwor).*

KF 746

In Sufi terminology, understanding is said to connote being at the point of having gnosis of the Divine Names and Attributes.

LG

Understanding represents the knowledge of things through the senses.

TJ

When he came to understand the infinity of the Essence,
He fell in love with his own understanding.

Maghrebi

FOLLY *(safah)*

Folly represents neglect of the Divine command.

KM 501

Folly represents the light-headedness that is the effect of joy or rage upon a person, causing him to commit acts that are contrary to reason and the religious law.

TJ

It would be far, far from his ocean-wide intellect
For madness to prompt him to commit folly!

MM II 1432

Loyalty turned to betrayal and cleverness to folly;
Friendship turned to hostility and humanity to oppression.

Sanā'i

FOOLISHNESS *(bolh)*

Whenever one who yearns for God is stripped and made destitute by intimacy [with God], God's Sanctity overwhelms him and he becomes distracted *(walah)* and bewildered in love. At this point, the pleasure of intimacy overcomes him and he loses control of his movements, as joy in God brings on the early stages of intoxication. He then passes from joy to delirium, and he has no consciousness of his spiritual state in his performance of devotions. This occurs to those who are subject to fluctuation *(talwin).*

The Prophet said, "It is the people of paradise who are more prone to foolishness." By paradise here the Prophet meant the paradise of witnessing *(jannat-e moshāhada).*

The gnostic said, "Foolishness means bewilderment in the wilderness of Union *(weṣāl).*"

MA 114

COMPREHENSION *(fahm)*

In Sufi terminology comprehension is to conceptualize the meaning of that which a speaker is explaining to one.

TJ

Comprehension is the means to perceive.

EE

Comprehension indicates perception of the inscrutable aspects of Divine mysteries and lights that precede the early stages of clear vision and revelation.

TT

Comprehension is the pearl of inspiration *(elhām).*

SS 634

Comprehension is the essence of reason as the kernel is to the nut.

LT 227

My head is lowered in the dust
before the winehouse;
Tell those who do not comprehend
to bang their heads against a brick wall.

Ḥāfeẓ

They all answered him
"We shall pledge our lives;
We shall summon up
and pool our comprehension."

MM I 46

The apprehensive faculty is frustrated
by the Essence's awesomeness.
Comprehension cannot maneuver
in striving to describe it.

HH 61

ELECT COMPREHENSION (*fahm-e khāṣṣ*)

Whenever an intimate of God comes to know Him, and perceives the realities of the dictates of the Unseen, he sees the reality of things in terms of their quiddity *(māhiyat),* in other words, as they really are, through one of the special lights shown to those who have become purified. According to the Koran: "And We caused Solomon to comprehend it." (XXI: 79)

The gnostic said, "Elect comprehension is where one comprehends something through elect inspiration without an angelic intermediary."

MA 239

APPREHENSIVE FACULTY(*wahm*)

The apprehensive faculty is one of the corporeal faculties of man, being located at the rear of the middle ventricle of the brain. Its function is the sensing of particular characteristics, such as the courage or generosity of someone. This is the faculty that causes the sheep to take flight from the wolf and the child to be given affection. This faculty governs all the other corporeal faculties, just as the intellect is served by all the other intellectual faculties.

TJ

The apprehensive faculty is the sentinel of comprehension.

SS 634

Certain Sufis maintain that Moḥammad's apprehensive faculty was the source of 'Azrā'il. God created Moḥammad's apprehensive faculty out of the light of His perfect Name and 'Azrā'il, in turn, out of the light of Moḥammad's apprehensive faculty. Having created the human apprehensive faculty out of the light of perfection, God presented it in the guise of wrath. The most powerful thing found in man is the apprehensive faculty. It dominates intellect, thought, and the faculty of conceptualization. By the same token, the most powerful of the angels is 'Azrā'il, for he was created out of the apprehensive faculty.

KF 1513

The apprehensive faculty is one of the lights of the Universal Intellect that descended into the lower world with the human spirit. Since it became far removed from the lights of the Intellect, it became reduced in scope and grew dim, and came to be called the apprehensive faculty. Thus, once the human constitution arrives at equilibrium, whereby the power of perception enjoyed by this faculty increases and its lights derive ever more from the Primal Source, it concentrates once more on the process of its perfection, becoming an intellect and perceiver of the whole.

NsN133

When Ebrāhim Khawwāṣ was asked about the apprehensive faculty, he explained, "It stands between intellect and comprehension, yet is neither related to, nor shares the attributes of either. Its intermediate position is like that of the light that stands between the sun and the water that reflects it, being of neither substance; nor like the state between sleep and wakefulness, where one is neither sleeping nor awake. It represents both the penetration and effect of the intellect upon understanding, and that of understanding upon intellect, for neither is superior to the other.

LT 226

Ebn 'Arabi was aware of the importance of the apprehensive faculty in the behavior of the Sufi's ego and the domination of imagination which reinforces this faculty in the ego, so that it is unable to separate one from the other. Therefore, imagination incites knowledge against apprehension, for knowledge is capable of breaking the grip of it by means of spiritual truths.

Ebn 'Arabi says that the apprehensive faculty is incapable of overcoming knowledge and obliterating it. This elucidates the importance of knowledge in combatting the apprehensive faculty and the necessity for alertness, so that apprehension may not be permitted to gain the upper hand over knowledge and keep it from functioning.

MjS 1241

Intellect is opposed
to the passions, O champion;
Whatever's involved with the passions --
Don't call it 'intellect'.

That which is a beggar of the passions,
call it apprehension;
Illusion is counterfeit, whereas the intellect
is coin of gold.

Apprehension and intellect cannot be
distinguished without a touchstone;
Bring them both immediately
to have a touchstone applied.

M IV 2301-2304

Illusion and opinion
are the bane
Of the particular intellect,
for it dwells in darkness.

MM III 1558

SENSATION *(ḥess)*

According to Sufi terminology, sensation is an attribute of the *nafs*. Its truth is the overpowering of the spirit through the nature of the *nafs* established in the heart.

Makki said, "Whoever claims to experience no sensation while undergoing the onslaught of a state is wrong. Absence of sensation can only be experienced through the senses, and experiencing or not experiencing states can only occur through the senses.

LT 348[1]

1. MA 566.

IMAGINATION *(khayāl)*

Imagination is the faculty that retains the sensible forms which the integrative sense *(ḥess-e moshtarek)*[1] perceives after materiality has disappeared, such that whenever the integrative sense is focused on imagination, it witnesses these forms. The imagination is the storehouse of the integrative sense, its location being the rear part of the anterior ventricle of the brain.

TJ

According to the most ancient of the sages of the soul, imagination is one of the five inward senses. Its function is that when something becomes apparent, or a person is seen, and the imagined form of the perceived object is retained, the object can be recalled in the mind at will without the object being before one's eyes; an object, for example, like a town which one has seen and left. Thus, the function of the imagination is to perceive the spiritual realities through the forms. Imagination may be thought of as an exegete who separates form from meaning. There must, first, be someone to create the text for there to be a meaning behind its expressions. Then the exegete can interpret the meaning in different words without having before his eyes the things that the original writer had seen. Of course, either his eye or another of his senses must be capable of sensing the meaning intended.

D

For God's intimates, imagination is the mirror of His Acts in the heart. This is the positive imagination that translates the forms of the Unseen into pleasing outward forms. Theophany of the Attributes often occurs in disguise in the imagination, which, in turn, transforms and manifests them in the raiment of beauty to intensify the nearness of the intimates and their love [for God]. This imagination brings peace from God to His prophets, emissaries and intimates, so that they may not be seared by the thrusts of the Might.

The gnostic said, "Imagination is the mirror of the lights of Beauty."

MA 182

---

1. A sense which integrates the information received from the other five sences, also called the *sensus comunus*. See Page 14 below.

You are robed in imagination
but You are the Truth.
You appear as imagination,
But You are everlasting

Mozzafar Ali Shah

According to Ebn 'Arabi, imagination churns things up like a productive flood, its governance extending to every realm of being. It enters the truth of all things. It shapes the intermediate realm *(barzakh)* which lies between the realm of spiritual realities and that of sensible things.

The reality of imagination is constantly changing, it may appear in any form. True Being, which is God, does not change. No being is realized except God, and whatever is other than God is changeable, imagination is no more than a vanishing shadow.

Nothing stays the same but God; everything else is continuously passing from one form to another; imagination is no more than this. The primal cloud *('amā')* is the substance of the whole universe, which itself appears only in the imagination.

MjS 449

According to Ebn 'Arabi, the universe is imagination; indeed, he goes further and refers to it as imagination upon imagination.

God's Being is co-existent with self-subsistent True Being *(wojud-e ḥaqiqi),* while the being of the universe is figurative, relative and transitory, a shadow of God's Being, upon which it is dependent. Consequently, its very essence is impermanent. In other words, it is illusion and imagination. Accordingly, Ebn 'Arabi considers the universe to be imagination, the quiddity *(māhiyat)* of which, in his view, may be defined as constant change and appearing in any form. From the point of view of his mystical doctrine, the universe is likewise in a state of constant change, transformation, motion and shifting; hence, it is imagination.

Sometimes Ebn 'Arabi ascribes another meaning to imagination, namely, 'that which displays things in a different form', although when one reflects on what one sees, one realizes what it really is.

Therefore, Ebn 'Arabi writes, "Those who are veiled by the darkness of ignorance and banned from the light of true gnosis are subject to the imagining or illusion that the universe enjoys true existence, self-subsistence and independence from God; this, in fact, is contrary to the actual situation. If one reflects deeply on the matter, one will realize that the existence of the universe is the very existence of God, which is manifested through the principal essences *(a'yān-e thābeṭa)* and their forms."

By imagination, Ebn 'Arabi does not mean the flimsy, insubstantial imagination that is a form of sickness and temptation, nor the imagination that is the philosophical term for the storehouse of the integrative sense, being located at the rear of the first chamber of the brain, nor the archetypal realm *('ālam-e khayāl),* as one of the five planes of existence, but something which, in philosophical terms, is extensive and embraces every plane and state so existential realities are displayed as symbolic forms within it — forms which themselves are subject to change.

Hence, according to Ebn 'Arabi, imagination constitutes all things that are manifested to the senses and the intellect in diverse forms that need to be interpreted in order for their realities to be known.

This is why Ebn 'Arabi calls life both dream and imagination, as well as imagination upon imagination, and considers True Being to be exclusively God, who is fixed and unchanging.

As has already been demonstrated, he is not content to consider the universe merely as imagination, but goes further, emphasizing that the existence of material being is imagination upon imagination, maintaining that the existence of the universe, including our own existence and our perceptive faculties, is imagination, nothing but a shadow. Furthermore, those relative existent things that we perceive are by their very nature impermanent, speculative, and mere imagination. Thus, from this, it stands to reason that the material existence we perceive is imagination upon imagination, or as Ḥāfeẓ puts it, nothing upon nothing:

The world with all that it involves
is nothing upon nothing;
I have verified this statement
a thousand times over.

Ebn 'Arabi expresses it this way: "So be advised that you are imagination, and everything that you claim to perceive as not being you is imagination upon imagination."[1]

1. FM 104.

This is to say that since it has been established that the existence of the universe is not True, but relative, and the sole True Being is God, one should be aware that one's self and one's perceptual faculties, as well as all that one perceives, including everything that is other than oneself, is imagination. Therefore, the whole of existence is imagination upon imagination where the first imagination denotes the whole universe, the shadow, while the second denotes the person being addressed as well as his perceptual faculties.

For Ebn 'Arabi, however, this imagination, this shadowy relative existence, is not totally empty, void or without foundation. One must not ignore it, but be aware that this dream has an interpretation. This notion, this imagination, has a foundation. This figurative thing has a True aspect, and this shadow has an Essence and a Possessor.

Just as we interpret our own dreams, so must we analyze and interpret this reality in a correct manner, while understanding that it is just a notion, a dream, an imagination. Through this understanding we may discover the reality of the phenomena of this universe beyond the outward forms, the imagined or dreamed existent things.

This is attested to by a Tradition of the Prophet: "People are asleep; when they die, they awaken."

While material existence is imagination,
it is God in Reality;
Whoever understands this comes to learn
the secrets of the Path.

To conclude, existence, in terms of external forms, is imagination, though an imagination that displays Reality. This Reality is God's Being, manifested in the external forms.

EA 316

The plane of imagination, including the forms that have taken shape there, is perfectly valid and corresponds to reality, provided that the influence upon imagination descends from the higher plane of the luminous heart, not from a lower plane. The reason for this lies in the process of descent that effects the lower planes, the universal spiritual reality of the Mother Book *(ommo'l-ketāb)* descends to the realm of the Guarded Tablet *(lauḥ-e maḥfuẓ)* which serves as the heart of the universe. From here it descends to the archetypal realm, where it takes shape and then down to the realm of the senses, where it is visualized. The realm of the senses is the fourth stage in the descent of existence from higher to lower, or inner to outer, or from the realm of Divine knowledge to that of material existence.

Human imagination is the dependent archetypal realm, just as the archetypal realm [in its own right] is absolute imagination or the imagination of the universe. Hence, human imagination is focused on the archetypal realm, on the one hand, for it belongs there and is joined to it; on the other hand, it is part of the *nafs* and the body of the individual.

Whatever becomes imprinted and displayed upon the imagination from a lower level of existence in a form to which the *nafs* or physical constitution of the individual may be related, rises like steam to the upper part of the brain, as the melancholic humor does with those of warm temperament. This imagination is not True, and is referred to as a confused dream. However, whatever descends to the imagination from a higher domain, either from the archetypal realm or from the luminous heart, and has taken form in the imagination, is True, whether viewed in sleep or a waking state.

NN 157

Existence, in terms of its being a shadow [of Reality], is imagination, whereas in terms of the Reality it is Being Itself, having assumed the diverse forms of the determined *(mota'ayyena)* essences and the names of phenomenal existent things.

RSh IV 513

If the veil were to fall
for an instant from His countenance,
The two worlds would appear
as playthings of imagination.

'Aṭṭār

He arrived from afar
like a crescent moon,
Non-existent, yet existing
in imaginational form.

In the spirit,
imagination is as nothing;
Yet see a world
proceeding in imagination!

Their peace and their war
are in imagination;
Their pride and their shame
are from imagination.

The imagined forms
which ensnare the friends of God
Are simply the reflections
of the fair ones in God's garden.
MM I 69-72

PURE REVELATION AND IMAGINATIONAL REVELATION *(kashf-e mojarrad wa kashf-e mokhayyal)*

The forms which take shape on the plane of imagination are of two kinds:

1) The external form adapts to that which the faculty of imagination *(qowwa-ye motakhayyala)* conceptualizes. Whatever it may be, it adapts to the imagination's conceptualization, whereby it is called pure revelation, that is to say, free of control by the faculty of imagination.

2) Where the conceptualization of imagination does not correspond to an external form, and the conceptualizing faculty has control, imposing an appropriate form thereon. Since it does not correspond to real form, some refer to this as imaginational revelation, as requiring interpretation, that is to say, transference from the viewed form to another expression [its fundamental reality].

NN 157

DISENGAGED IMAGINATION *(khayāl-e mojarrad)*

Disengaged imagination occurs when base thoughts dominate the heart and separate the spirit from vision of the Unseen. When one is in a state of dreaming or between sleep and wakefulness, this imagination grows more powerful. The faculty of true imagination covers each thought in an imaginal guise so the actual forms of the thoughts are witnessed without interference by the individual's false faculty of imagination, thus allowing the separation to be detected and observed. An example of disengaged imagination is the case of one who is obsessed with the thought of finding a treasure, so he dreams of discovering it. The master knows that this is the effect of a desire which has taken form within the dreamer and can only repudiate its validity by calling it a false representation of true imagination.

When such a representation occurs in dreams, it is known as a confused dream *(aḍhghātho'l-aḥlām)*, and if it occurs in reality, it is referred to as a false event. In representations of this nature, truth is never involved, for the *nafs* independently and without the cooperation of the spirit is the source of such thoughts, and truth is far removed from the attributes of the *nafs*.

There are two conditions for the truth of an event: one must be immersed in remembrance *(dhekr)* and absent from sensible things, and there must be sincerity and detachment of the inner consciousness *(serr)* from contemplation of what is other than God. It is possible for disengaged imagination to turn into revelation of imagination for the sincere one, where, due to one's immersion in remembrance and the Divine presence, the spirit of unveiling *(kashf)* becomes formed into the shape of imagination, whereby the form of an event comes about, being capable of interpretation.

MH 175

THE ABSOLUTE, REALIZED, DISCONTIGUOUS, AND CONTIGUOUS IMAGINATION *(khayāl-e moṭlāq, khayāl-e moḥaqqeq, khayāl-e monfaṣel, khayāl-e mottaṣel)*

Ebn 'Arabi divides imagination into four categories: absolute, realized, discontiguous and contiguous.

The absolute imagination is the primal cloud *('amā')*, the all-comprehensive plane and has the potential to receive all forms of the universe.

The realized imagination is the absolute imagination after it has received the forms of the universe.

The discontiguous imagination is a realm [in the hierarchy of being] with its own independent existence, manifesting sensations that are separate to the imagining observer, as in the case of the Prophet's conceptualization of Gabriel in the face of Daḥyā Kalbi.

The contiguous imagination is the faculty of imagination of an individual who possesses the power to conceptualize forms.

MjS 449

Having descended from the level of spirits, existence descends to that of archetypes *(methāl)*, which serves as an intermediate plane between the realm of spirits and the realm of corporeal entities. Some philosophers call this the archetypal realm, giving it the theological designation of *barzakh* (intermediate realm).

However, according to the realized ones *(moḥaqqeq)*, the archetypal or intermediate plane is something separate. Some of them believe that the brain must be involved in its perception and refer to it as the dependent imagination, a realm in which dreams and fantasies exist. Others maintain that the brain does not have a role in the perception of it and refer to it as the discontiguous imagination, that which manifests the embodiment of spirits and the spiritualization of bodies, the individualization of conscience and behavior, the manifestation of spiritual realities in appropriate forms, and the witnessing of incorporeal entities in corporeal form.

NN 52

THE DEPENDENT IMAGINATION AND THE ABSOLUTE IMAGINATION
(khayāl-e moqayyad wa khayāl-e moṭlāq)

Absolute imagination is dependent upon the absolute archetypal realm *('ālam-e methāl-e moṭlāq)* and is accessible to anyone. Whoever observes this dependency will find the Way to the Absolute, where, in perceiving the subtleties of what is derivative, one is made aware of the Principle. Of course, Ebn 'Arabi did not discuss the plane of the absolute imagination, mentioning that of the dependent only briefly. He stated, "Know that the plane of the imagination, that is to say, the level that encompasses the forms that have been foreshadowed in the faculty of imagination and is joined to created human nature, along with whatever is imagined, is also known as a dependent archetype in the way that the archetypal realm is called the absolute imagination, its relationship to the archetypal plane being that of streams to the great rivers of which they are branches."

The plane of the imagination is all-inclusive, embracing every object possessing external existence and every non-object that exists within it, that is to say, all that exists and is non-existent.

The plane of the imagination gives form to everything, that is, every unit of existence or non-existence, and is able to present them to the *nafs* in sensible forms, whether in dreams, as is the case for people in general, or in an awakened state, as is the case for certain individuals, whether they be absent to the senses or not.

NN 156

MEMORY *(ḥāfeẓa)*

Memory is a faculty that is located in the posterior ventricle of the brain. Its function is to take note of the particular meanings that the estimative faculty perceives. It is the storehouse of the apprehensive faculty, in the same way that the imagination is for the primal sense. The memory is also known as the reminder, because it reminds one of things.

RSh I 358

THE INTEGRATIVE SENSE *(ḥess-e moshtarak)*

The integrative sense is the faculty in which the particular forms of sensible things are identified. The five external senses serve as its spies, and inform the *nafs* of these forms so that it may perceive them. Its location is the front chamber of the brain. It is like a wellspring from which flow five streams.

TJ

THE IMAGINATIVE FACULTY *(motakhayyala)*

The imaginative faculty has control over both sensible forms and the particular meanings that are separated from these forms. It governs both composite and disassembled objects, being able, for example, to conceptualize both a man with two heads and a man with no head at all. Whenever this faculty is in the service of the intellect, it is called the reflective faculty *(mofakkara);* if apprehension engages it to perceive sensible things, it is called the imaginative faculty.

TJ

DEDUCTION *(estenbāṭ)*

Deduction involves the rigorous mental extraction of meanings from texts; it is performed by the inventive faculty *(qowwa-ye qariḥa).*

TJ

Deduction represents the extraction of philosophical wisdom from the Koran and the Customs of the Prophet *(sonnat).*

SS 634

Whenever the veils covering the brides of the spiritual sciences are lifted in front of God's chosen one in the bridal chambers of wisdom, a thousand or more meanings pour out, for the observer is of the elect of the people of God.

The gnostic said, "The brides of the truths of knowledge are unveiled only for God's chosen ones.

MA

PERCEPTION *(edrāk)*

In Sufi terminology perception represents the full comprehension of something, and involves apprehension of the form of that thing in the rational soul (*nafs-e nāṭeqa*). The representation of the reality of a thing without involvement of reason, whether in denial or affirmation thereof, is called conceptualization. If reason is involved, be it in denial or affirmation, it is known as attestation *(taṣdiq)*.

TJ

No one sees You
as You are;
Each perceives
according to his own insight.

Ḥāfeẓ

THE ULTIMATE PERCEPTION *(edrāk-e edrāk)*

Perception involves knowledge that engenders compulsory worship and elicits God's general mercy. Ultimate perception involves knowledge that engenders voluntary worship, traversal of the Path, and elicits God's special mercy.

HY 10

The extreme limit of knowledge, namely ultimate perception, is non-perception, for the True Perceived One has no limitation, whereas knowledge is limited. This non-perception entails no perception of perceiving. Non-perception entails the bewilderment and immersion of the perceiver in the Perceived. When one is in a state of non-perception, one will appear to be ignorant and heedless. That is to say, one who experiences this state becomes hidden to the eyes of the world.

Upon attaining this state, the perceiver's true nature, hidden from the world of multiplicity and pluralism, becomes elevated and subsequently annihilated in the Perceived One. Perception, insofar as it exists, is manifested in the perceiver who comes to experience, "The day when the earth will change to other than the earth," (XIV: 48) and "the day when we shall roll up the heavens as a recorder rolleth up a written scroll." (XXI: 104), and all that accompanies this, such as the scattering of the stars, the overthrowing of the sun, and so forth. Then the true everlasting call will reach the wayfarer's unconscious ear, saying, "Whose is the sovereignty this day?" (X: 16), and from the void of true annihilation will come the reply: "It is God's, the One, the Almighty." (XL: 16)

HY 11

What is the relationship
between the material and spiritual realms?
When perception
is incapable of perceiving perception.

Shabestari

THE PERCEPTION OF UNIVERSAL KNOWLEDGE *(edrāk-e 'elm-e kolli)*

Whenever the spirit of one experiencing Divine Unity sips the cool water of Divine knowledge drawn from the sea of the realities of things, it proceeds to swim in the ocean of Eternity and post-eternity and dives to the depths of the sea of the Divine Identity from which it emerges with the Attributes of Oneness *(aḥadiyat)*. Thereupon, it comes to know all that is the object of knowledge and all that is known and unknown. At this point, the cognition of every cause is revealed to it, and it comes to know the internal aspect of the Divine Acts and of the realities of things.

The Prophet stated, "Indeed, only the one who knows through God knows anything of the hidden form of God's knowledge."

The gnostic said, "Whenever the gnostic comes to know the universal, nothing remains hidden from him, for whenever the morning of Union dawns, all that lies hidden becomes manifest in its radiance, and all knowledge and knowable things are revealed by its lights.

MA 205

EXPERIENCING PERCEPTION *(estedrāk)*

Whenever the spiritual realities of the morning of pre-eternity are manifested to God's chosen one, he comes to experience those high states that had passed from him, ascending thereto by the stairway of stations of nearness [to God].

The gnostic said, "Experiencing perception is reality for observers with vision."

MA 268

INTENTION *(niyat)*

Intention is a resolve born of gnosis, possessing the power to stimulate action. It has three levels: 1) the pure, which stirs one to desire nothing but encounter with God; 2) the turbid, which causes one to be hypocritical, seeking rank and the world; 3) intermixed *(momtazāj)*, which has many levels: "For all there will be ranks from what they did." (VI: 132)

KF 440

Some maintain that intention means the resolve to act, while others hold that it means thinking about the sort of action which one may undertake. Jonaid said, "Intention is the conceptualization of actions." Another has said, "The believer's intention is God."

LT

If you should see a head
in the doorway of the winehouse,
Do not step on it, for that
may not be God's intention.

Ḥāfeẓ

One who sees the foam
forms intentions,
While one who sees the Sea
makes his heart the Sea.

MM V 2909

RESOLVE *('azm)*

Resolve means to make the will firm. It becomes one's inclination after one has resisted inducements stimulated by ideas from the intellect, by the passions or by tricks of the *nafs*. If none of the contending ideas prevail, then one becomes bewildered, whereas if one idea dominates, resolve is required. Resolve is a quality of the *nafs*.

KF

In the early stages, resolve is required to follow the rules of the shar'iat, while in the final stages, it actualizes God's will, where the state of actualization presupposes one's subsistence in God. "And you do not will, unless God wills." (LXXVI: 30)

RSh IV 176

With resolve to behold You
the soul reached its limit;
Should it live or should it die?
What is Your command?

Ḥāfeẓ

Mount the steed
of resolve,
For true resolve
is the Buraq.

Maghrebi

Your states, like letters,
are His transcribing;
Your resolve to change
are from His resolve and changing.

MM III 2781

According to the Koran: "And when you are resolved, then put your trust in God." (III: 159)

Resolve means to actualize one's purpose, whether willingly or not. It has three degrees:

1) The rejection of knowledge having observed the lightning of visionary revelation. Here, one desires that the light of intimacy be lasting and consents to mortify the passions.

2) The desire to drown in the radiance of witnessing, to seek splendor in the illumination of the Path, and to gather the forces of constancy.

3) The recognition of the defectiveness of resolve, followed by the resolve to be liberated from it, followed by giving up the effort to abandon. Resolutions provide those who hold them with the most precious inheritance, namely, the ability to perceive the defectiveness of their own resolve.

MS

The Twenty-seventh Field is that of Resolve, which is born of the Field of Return to God. According to the Koran: "Then have patience, [O Moḥammad], as those with resolve amongst the emissaries had patience." (XLVI: 35)

Resolve means cutting off what ever is other than the desired thing and turning the heart away from everything else.

Resolve means correcting one's aim and possessing a pure and collected heart. It involves three points:

1) The resolve to repent from transgression, ridding one's self of the motivation for transgression, and breaking off association with bad companions.

2) The resolve to serve, being prepared to execute a command even before it is given, to perform one's obligatory practice at the prescribed time, and to give priority to religion over that of the world.

3) The resolve with respect to Reality, which consists of calm in time of anger, generosity in time of need, and modesty in time of endurance.

The basis of resolve is threefold: 1) firmness in religion, 2) zealous fidelity to God's commands, and 3) constancy in the spiritual moment.

SM

The gnostic's resolve is to attain sacred subtleties from the transitory and eternal realm, and to be characterized by God's Attributes after his annihilation in the resplendence of assaults by the Essence. Upon attainment, he becomes established in the vision of the grandeur of God's Majesty and Beauty. God told his Prophet, who had plunged into the seas of the Splendor, "Then have patience, as those with resolve amongst the emissaries had patience." (XLVI: 35)

The gnostic said, "Resolve is the severing of attachments while proceeding towards attainment to God."

MA 143

The resolve of the adherent to Divine Unity is to attain the station of the perfected ones amongst the prophets and friends of God. It signifies tolerance of infusions that emanate from the pre-eternal Will through the vision of Uniqueness, as well as stability and constancy, free of human agitation and display at the station of exhilaration. In describing those of His emissaries who possessed resolve whilst inspiring His cherished Prophet towards that station, God said, "Have patience, as those with resolve amongst the emissaries had patience." (XLVI: 35)

The gnostic said, "Resolve is to welcome God as the Beloved with constancy and joy in His everlasting Beauty."

MA 208

PURPOSE *(qaṣd, qoṣud)*

In the early stages, purpose represents detachment from the world for the sake of spiritual practice, while in the final stages, it is obliteration in God through the essence of Concentration as well as liberation from the conventions of the creation.

RSh IV 176

Purpose is to risk your life
for the lips of the Beloved;
See how I strive
to bring this about!

Ḥāfeẓ

According to the Koran, "And whoever leaves his home, for the cause of God and His Prophet, and death overtakes him, his reward is, then, incumbent on God." (IV: 100)

The wayfarer's purpose is removed from worshipping anything but God. It is of three degrees:

1) The purpose that urges one to austerity, liberating one from irresolution, and invites one to put aside self-interested motives.

2) The purpose that cuts away any secondary cause which one may confront, prevents any obstacle that may come along from getting in the way, and eases any difficulty one may encounter.

3) The purpose that directs the devotee to submit utterly, so that he may be purified by God's knowledge, trampled by God's decree, and thrown into the sea of annihilation.

MS

The Sixth Field is that of Purpose, which arises from the Field of Devotion *(erādat)*. Correctness of purpose and honesty of intention are the seeds of action, according to the Koranic passage: "And whoever leaves his home, for the cause of God and His Prophet, and death overtakes him, his reward is incumbent on God." (IV: 100)

Purpose means making God the goal, abandoning everything other than Him. There are three basic kinds of purpose:

1) Bodily purpose through service, which has three indications: unrelenting endeavour, the minimizing of material pleasure, and the

seeking of release.

2) Purpose of heart through gnosis, which has three indications: the undergoing of suffering, the choosing of solitude, and basic subsistence.

3) Purpose of soul through suffering, which has three indications: being sensitive of heart, not being content with audition *(samā')*, and desiring death.

SM

The spirit's purpose is to seek through worship the sacred motherlode from which it has emerged. The heart's purpose is to attain through worship that which pleases the heart such as visionary revelations from the Unseen. The purpose of the inner consciousness is directed from the core of the heart to the realm of joys, for the core of the heart is the site of the circulation of the inner consciousness of the sincere ones, within who blow the winds of Union across the deserts of nearness [to God]. According to the Koran: "And God's is the purpose of the Way." (XV: 9)

The gnostic said, "Purpose is the stirring of the human nature to power."

MA 28

Purpose represents the application of worship based on sincere intentions that accompany movement towards one's goal.

It is related that Aḥmad ebn 'Aṭā' said, "If amongst all the possibilities of purposes one chooses that which is directed towards something other than God, one is delivering the greatest affront to God."

Wāseṭi said, "To direct one's purposes towards incoming thoughts *(khāṭer)* [that is, God's communications] is to ignore the Worshipped One Himself. How can anyone whose attention is on the communications of God witness His purposes? This is to say that anyone who in framing his purpose, desires the object of the purpose is not conscious of the purpose itself."

LT 369

By purpose the Sufis mean correctness of resolve *('azm)* in seeking the reality of the Object of purpose. Purpose for the Sufis is not dependent on motion and rest, for although a lover may be at rest in love, he is still pursuing a purpose. This is contrary to the normal situation, where for those who pursue a purpose it affects them either outwardly or inwardly; whereas lovers pursue their purpose without being affected by either their seeking or their movements, all their attributes being directed in purpose towards the Beloved.

KM 505

Purpose means devotion with sincere intention linked with the wayfarer's action. Its reality is the activity of the inner consciousness in vying and longing to contemplate the Eternal.

SS 623

REMEMBRANCE *(dhekr)*

In Sufi terminology, remembrance refers to the remembering of God, whether vocally or in the heart.

Since Your grace has been watching over me,
what fear is there of boldness?
Since remembrance of You is present,
what dread is there of lapses?

Sanā'i

Nuri said, "Remembrance is where the one who remembers becomes absent in remembrance."

Dho Nun said, "Remembrance is the being of the Remembered."

TSA 193

In the early stages, remembrance is outward, while in the final stages we become aware of God's remembrance of us and become liberated from our own remembrance of Him. Here, annihilation of the one who remembers in the Remembered occurs, where God becomes the Remembered, remembrance, and the one who remembers.

RSh IV 177

When Abu Sa'id Abe'l-Khair was asked the meaning of the passage: "But, indeed, the remembrance of God is more important" (XXIX: 45), he explained, "It means it is greater if God remembers the devotee, because the devotee cannot remember Him until He remembers the devotee first. What is greater is that God remembers the devotee, bringing the devotee into harmony, that he may remember God.

AT 313

Abu Sa'id Abe'l-Khair said, "Remembrance is to forget everything but God."

AT 297

Naṣrābādi said, "The reality of remembrance is that the one who remembers becomes absent from his remembrance in the witnessing of the Remembered. Thus, through witnessing the Remembered One, the one who remembers becomes absent from consciousness of himself. At this point, God is witnessing Himself."

TSA 63

Wāseṭi said, "Remembrance occurs in both absence and presence. When the absent one is absent from himself and present in God, his remembrance is witnessing, and when he is absent from God and present with himself it is not remembrance but absence, and absence arises from heedlessness."

TA 734

THE DIFFERENT LEVELS OF REMEMBRANCE *(anwā' wa marāteb-e dhekr)*

Remembrance is said to involve the presence of the True Remembered One with the one who remembers. According to the realized ones, this remembrance has several levels:

1) Outward remembrance is where the Remembered is present in outward, vocal expression through the senses and heart of the one who remembers while observing spiritual practice and heart-adherence, as opposed to the heedless of heart who "forgot God, therefore He caused them to forget their souls." (LIX: 19).

Remembrance of You on my tongue works like sugar.
Your Name on my tongue is like a drop on a dewy leaf.

2) Inward remembrance is where the Remembered One is involved, while the one who remembers is oblivious of his own existence, where he "a thing unrememberd." (LXXVI: 1) At this level, remembrance is inward and is practised by the tongue of the heart.

God knows that I cannot remember Him,
For how can I remember one I can't forget?

3) Remembrance of the Remembered involves both the Remembered One and the absence of the one who remembers, who forgets

his own being. In this case, remembrance involves realization of the True Being of the Remembered One on the part of the transitory remembrance of the lover, who, in terms of the promise of "Remember Me, that I remember you," (II: 152), is transformed from a lost self that remembers the Beloved to one who enjoys His remembrance and who says:

"How can I forget My lover, who even
In separation is still in My embrace!"

TT

According to the Koran: "Remember your Lord, when you forget," (XVIII: 24), that is, when you forget what is other than Him and when you forget yourself in the course of your remembrance, then you forget your remembrance in the course of your remembrance. Finally you forget all remembrance in God's remembrance. Remembrance is liberation from heedlessness and forgetting. It is of three degrees:

1) Outer, which consists of praise, prayer, and observance.

2) Inner, which involves being liberated from flagging, remaining in witnessing, and persisting in nightly communion.

3) True, which is the witnessing of God's remembrance and involves being liberated from being conscious of remembrance, and being aware of the fact that every one who remembers who is conscious of his own remembrance is subject to flagging.

MS 118

Remembrance is of three kinds, based respectively on habit *('ādat)*, accounting *(ḥesbat)*, and association *(ṣoḥbat)*.

Remembrance based on habit has no value, for it involves heedlessness [of God]. Remembrance based on accounting has no virtue, for it is merely the seeking of reward. Remembrance based on association is something held in trust, for the tongues of those who remember are on loan. The remembrance of the one who fears is in dread of estrangement; that of one who hopes, in expectation of gaining the object of his seeking; that of the lover, from the agony of burning. The first fearfully hears a threatening voice [from God] and falls to prayer. The second hopefully hears a promising voice [from God] and falls to praising. The third lovingly hears an encouraging voice and proceeds without pretext. The gnostic received the pre-eternal remembrance and gave up all efforts, leaving things to change.

KAM I 550

There are three kinds of remembrance: that which is vocal, that of the heart, and that of the soul. The vocal is based on habit and that of the heart on worship, while that of the soul is a sign of bliss.

One who is in the corporeal realm engages in remembrance based on habit; one in the realm of the Attributes remembers God in worship; and one who is immersed in the Essence remembers Him in the soul.

However, true remembrance is where the scripture is forgotten and the clarification brought by the light of Divine mission *(resālat)* is made manifest.

"And remember your Lord, when you forget." (XVIII: 24) This means that one should absolutely forget the attributes of human nature and consign oneself to non-existence, then drinking the wine of remembrance of God. Remembering the Beloved while conscious of oneself is neglectfulness *(ṣahw),* for the one who truly remembers is effaced *(maḥw)* in his remembrance. If there is any sign of the one who truly remembers, this is a deficiency, making him a pluralist at this level. When one remembers the Beloved, one must let one's self go. When one remembers, one must do so without thought of oneself, being characterized by the Eternal, so that one's attribution of existence turns to non-existence with no sign of oneself.

RAj 117

VOCAL AND SILENT REMEMBRANCE
(dhekr-e jali wa dhekr-e khafi)

Vocal remembrance is said to be that which is spoken, while the silent rememberance is said to be without speech.

***

One day in Jonaid's assembly Shebli cried, "Allāh!" Jonaid said, "If God is absent, remembrance of Him as absent is absence, and absence is profane. On the other hand, if God is present while one enjoys witnessing of him as present, one who calls His Name is violating sanctity."

TA 428

According to Moḥammad ebn Faḍhl: "Vocal remembrance

brings about the purgation of sins and the attainment of higher degrees. Silent remembrance in the heart brings about nearness to God."

TSS 210

Vocal remembrance is for the ordinary, while that of the heart is for the elect, being the first result of loving-kindness. This occurs when the heart gains insight through witnessing God's Attributes, with the gnostic's inner consciousness being stirred by loving-kindness, such that he finds peace in intimacy [with God], which leads to serenity for him. According to the Koran: "Indeed, in remembrance of God do hearts find rest!" (XIII: 28), which is the highest form of worship, as in the passage: "But indeed, remembrance of God is more important." (XXIX: 45) The Prophet stated, "The best remembrance is silent," that is, remembrance of the heart. According to the Koran: "Indeed, therein is a reminder for one who has a heart." (L: 37)

Nuri said, "Remembrance means the annihilation of the one who remembers in the Remembered."

The gnostic said, "Remembrance is a light struck from God's theophany to attract the hearts of gnostics to the loving-kindness of its purity."

MA 139

Whenever God's vicegerent becomes perfect in gnosis and perpetuation of the purity of his heart's remembrance, he does not become darkened by change in state, which involves mostly an alternation between contraction and expansion. He stops uttering remembrance and glorification *(tasbiḥ)* as God wills; or if his state is such, he chants remembrance and glorification like a child.

The gnostic said, "Vocal remembrance distances heedlessness from the heart. The vicegerent has no heedlessness in him".

MA 287

One day Bāyazid found himself less involved in his remembrance than usual. When he was asked about this, he replied, "I find this spoken remembrance strange. I find it stranger that it is so alien! What need is there for this alien for my remembrance is within my soul. It is alien because the very remembrance of Him is alien, standing between soul and Soul."

KAM I 420

Remembrance is a treasure, a treasure better hidden;
Strive to make your utterance of remembrance hidden!
Become mute of tongue, silent of lip;
There is no ear privy to this exchange.
Say it concealed in heart and in soul,
So that Satan may not find it out with wiles.
Keep the nafs *from knowing of it,*
So that it may not become proud.

Do not be revealed to angel either;
Otherwise, he'll make the secret public.
He will seek to immortalize it
By writing it down in the ledger of virtues.

HAu 20

IMITATIVE REMEMBRANCE *(dhekr-e taqlid)*

Imitative remembrance is that which is vocally communicated and received by the outer ear. Anybody can utter it. Remembrance of this nature has been likened to a seed lying in the earth which has not germinated. It has a difficult time ahead if it is ever to bear fruit.

***

REALIZING REMEMBRANCE *(dhekr-e taḥqiqi)*

Realizing remembrance is that which is inculcated and under the control of a friend of God, that is, a Perfect Master. It is planted in the fertile soil of the disciple's heart, developing under the gardener's care, tended and watered until it bears fruit.

***

THE CIRCLE OF REMEMBRANCE *(ḥalqa-ye dhekr)*

The circle of remembrance is said to represent the assembly of Sufis who are remembering God inwardly and outwardly in the presence of the master or a shaikh and observing a specified etiquette.

***

The heart is engaged in the circle of remembrance
Hoping that the circle of the tresses of multiplicity
Will be removed from the face of the Beloved.

Ḥāfeẓ

RECOLLECTION *(tadhakkor)*

Recollection signifies the *nafs's* attention to known forms in such a way that, whenever it wants, it may have easy access to them by way of an historically ingrained process.

NF

When conceptualization is acquired
By the heart, it may be termed 'recollection'.

Shabestari

In the early stages, recollection means accepting spiritual counsel, seeking direct vision, and seeking to be present with that which one has grasped through reflection. In the final stages, it means referring back to what one has experienced in annihilation.

RSh IV 171

The Thirtieth Field is Recollection, which derives from that of Consideration *(tafakkor)*. According to the Koran: "None recollects, save the one who turns to God contrite." (XL: 13) Recollection is the sign of the acceptance of something that one has received.

The difference between consideration and recollection is that the former involves seeking, while the latter has to do with finding.

There are three kinds of recollection:

1) Fearfully heeding the call of the Divine threat, which involves three things: terror of what is veiled of things past, dread of the unseen outcome, and regret over wasted moments.

2) Looking hopefully upon the announcer of the promise of the Friend, which involves three things: earnest repentance, attentive intercession and radiant mercy.

3) Responding to Divine beneficence with expression of neediness, which involves three things; constant nightly conversation *(monājāt)*, pre-eternal acquaintanceship that causes joy to burst forth, and a heart opened to viewing God.

SM

According to the Koran: "None recollects save the one who turns to God contrite." (XL: 13) Recollection is the sign of the acceptance of something that one has received.

Recollection is higher than consideration, for the latter involves seeking, while the former has to do with finding. The foundations of recollection are threefold:

1) Profiting from spiritual counsel, which comes once three things have come about: intense need for this, blindness to the faults of the advisor, and the recollection of God's promise and threat.

2) Drawing insight from lessons, which accompanies three things: the life of the intellect, the awareness of days, and the putting aside of self-interest.

3) Garnering the fruit of reflection *(fekr)*, which comes with three things: the curtailing of expectations, meditation on the Koran, and the minimizing of social life, desires, attachments, eating and sleep.

MS

THE DIFFERENCE BETWEEN REMEMBRANCE AND RECOLLECTION *(farq miān-e dhekr wa tadhakkor)*

Jonaid said, "The reality of remembrance is annihilation in the Remembered One. Remembrance is not a matter of simply mechanically moving the lips of one's own volition; this is recollection, which is affectation. True remembrance is where it is the heart which does all the speaking, and is itself taken to the level of the inner consciousness, which, in turn, becomes the fountainhead of witnessing, as the sources of dispersion are cut off. Full attention in the realm of Unity with God appears at this station, such that it has been said that when theophany is properly realized, then tongue, heart and inner consciousness become one. As remembrance becomes the Remembered at the level of the inner consciousness and the soul becomes light there, so communication turns to direct vision, which is far from verbal explanation."

KAM V 684

REFLECTION *(fekr)*

Reflection is said to mean organizing what is known, in order that one may attain what is unknown.

TJ 127

What is reflection?
Having the mysteries of the universe resolved,
Digging a mountain
out of the heart and becoming as a mustard seed.

MN 41

Reflection is that which opens a way; the Way is one on which a spiritual king advances.

The King is he who is king in himself, not one who is made king by treasuries and armies.

MM II 3207-3208

Reflection is said to mean becoming effaced in remembrance of God.

LG

In the terminology of the wayfarers, reflection means the traveling of the wayfarer on a voyage of removing the veils of multiplicity and determined forms *(ta'ayyon)* which are void from the point of view of Reality, that is to say, non-existent towards God, that is, in the direction of the Unity of Absolute Being, which is Reality. This traveling involves the wayfarer's attaining the station of annihilation in God and the effacement, the obliteration, of the essence of phenomenal existence in the light of the Unity of the Essence, as a drop is effaced in the sea.

KF 1123

You have your tree of paradise;
I'll stick with the Beloved's stature;
Everyone's reflection is according to his aspiration.

Ḥāfeẓ

Tājo'd-Din ebn 'Aṭā'o'llāh said, "Reflection is of two categories: one which springs from affirmation and faith, and one which springs from contemplative and direct vision. The first is particular to those concerned with transitory knowledge, while the second relates to those involved in insight and contemplative vision."

TKQ 761

CONSIDERATION *(tafakkor)*

Consideration is the heart's handling of the spiritual realities for the sake of perceiving the Sought One. It is the lamp by which the heart distinguishes between what is good and what is bad for it, and what is to its interest and to its detriment. A heart not involved in consideration steps forth in darkness.

Consideration has been described as the summoning up of the recognition of things which lie in the heart; the purifying of the heart by means of infused blessings entering therein; a lamp to guide one away from the transitory and a key to open the way out of personal volition; a garden full of the trees of spiritual truths and the milieu of the lights of nuances; the meadow of Reality and the riverbed of the religious law; the viewing of the annihilation of the world, its non-existence, and the weighing of the subsistence of the hereafter; and a trap for the bird of wisdom.

TJ 88

O You Who told us not to follow the pure ones of the age,
Where are we in this sea of consideration; where are You?

Sa'di

Consideration means going from what is void to the Truth,
Perceiving the Absolute Whole within the part.

Shabestari

In the early stages, consideration means insight through perception based on need, while in the final ones it means being transported from gnosis to realization, from form to spiritual reality, and from creation to God. Consideration of Yourself suffices you.

RSh IV 170

Moḥāsebi said, "Consideration is to see secondary causes through God, upon Whom they are based."

TA 273

Abu 'Amr Nojaid said, "Whoever observes consideration in the truest sense speaks truly and acts purely."

TSS 480

Whenever the gnostic's heart becomes situated in the valleys of the Acts, in the course of seeking the lights of the Attributes, God manifests to it through every goodness from the light of His Grace and through every evil from the mystery of the magnificence of His Wrath. This is consideration, which moves around the spirit in the angelic realm *(malakut)*. According to the Koran: "And consider the creation of the heavens and the earth: (III: 191) Consideration is the basis of worship, for it is worship of the heart, its virtue and its location. The Prophet said, "An hour's consideration is better than seventy years of worship."[1]

1. See the author's *Traditions of the Prophet,* New York, 1983, Vol. II.

Dho'n-Nun said, "Whoever devotes his heart to consideration comes to perceive the Unseen."

The gnostic said, "Consideration is the roaming of hearts amongst the Unseen."

MA 139

The Twenty-ninth Field is Consideration, which proceeds from that of Constancy *(esteqāmat).* Consideration is for the heart what analysis is for the nafs. Consideration is the ordering of known things to lead to that which is unknown. According to the Koran: "Such similitudes coin We for mankind that happly they may reflect." (LIX: 21)

Consideration is of three categories:

1) Prohibited, which involves consideration of three things: God's Attributes, leading to consternation; whether God will reward or punish one, leading to suspicion [of God]; and the mysteries of creation, leading to antagonism.

2) Recommended, which is of God's works, leading to wisdom; God's apportionment, leading to insight; and God's bounties, leading to loving-kindness.

3) Obligatory, which is of one's own efforts, leading to veneration; seeking out one's faults in spiritual practice, leading to shame; and the full purpose in what one has resolved to undertake, viewed in the light of one's caution, leading to fear.

Further obligatory consideration is of the cultivation of neediness, the reward of which is the beholding of God; this involves three things:

a) Consideration itself, which concerns one's doing, how one does it, and the fact that it should be done well.

b) Pondering *(tadabbor),* which concerns one's saying, what one says, and the fact that it should be said sincerely.

c) Recollection *(tadhakkor),* which concerns one's giving, how much one gives, and the fact that it should be pure.

SM

According to the Koran: "And We have sent to you, [Moḥammad], the Remembrance [Koran], that you might explain to the people what has been revealed for them, and that perhaps they might consider." (XVI: 44)

Know that consideration is inquiry by insight towards attainment of what is sought, and it is of three kinds:

1) Of the essence of Divine Unity, which means plunging into the sea of denial, from which one may be saved only by the safeguard of seizing the radiance of visionary revelation *(kashf)*, while adhering to the exoteric.

2) Of the subtleties of God's works, which water the seed of wisdom.

3) Of the meaning of devotional actions and spiritual states, which eases the passage along the Way of Reality.

Salvation from consideration of the essence of Divine Unity involves three things: being aware of the impotence of the intellect, ceasing to place hope in dwelling on goals, and the safeguard of seizing onto the handhold of veneration.

Perception in consideration of the subtleties of God's works involves three things: looking well upon the origins of Divine beneficence, answering the calls made through Divine intimations, and being delivered from the bondage of the passions.

Comprehension in consideration of the degrees of actions and states involves three things: seeking knowledge as one's companion, being wary of conventions, and knowing the places where productive rain falls.

MS

THE DIFFERENCE BETWEEN REFLECTION AND CONSIDERATION *(farq miān-e fekr wa tafakkor)*

When Ḥāreth Moḥāsebi was asked about reflection, he replied, "Reflection has to do with the subsistence of things in God. Some have said that consideration involves association with what is transitory, and others say that reflection is that which fills hearts with the state of veneration for God. The difference between reflection and consideration is that in the latter case the heart is roaming about, while in the former, the heart has arrived at comprehension of that with which it is acquainted."

LT 230

THOUGHT *(fekrat)*

Thought is the product of consideration, being the realization of certitude through pre-eternalness *(azaliyat)* and the Godhead *(oluhiyat);* and this realization, in turn, stems from consideration and sorrow *(ḥozn),* as well as fear of God. Moḥammad 'Ali Kattāni said, "Sorrowful sounds are stirred up from the fields of thought."

The gnostic said, "Thought represents the massing of the cloud of anxieties in the heart wounded by gnosis."

MA 139

Kharaqāni said, "One who does the ritual prayers and observes the fast is close to the creation, whereas one who enjoys thought is close to God."

TA 708

Moḥammad ebn Ḥāmed Termedhi said: "Thought is of five kinds: concerning God's signs, from which gnosis arises; concerning God's bounties, from which loving-kindness arises; concerning God's promise, as well as merit and reward, from which arises desire in the course of spiritual practice and obedience; concerning God's threat and His torment, from which arises fear of disobedience; and concerning the ungratefulness of the *nafs* in the face of God's beneficence towards one, from which arises awareness of one's past actions and shame before God.

TSS 297

A ray of light shines from the pavilions of His Majesty
From the Grandeur which transcends knowing thought.

Sa'di

Thought becomes confounded by Your subtle Essence;
Through Your Eternal knowledge, hidden things are known.

Sanā'i

Without brain and heart they were full of thought, without army and battle they gained victory.

That direct vision in relation to them is thought; otherwise, indeed, in relation to those who are far from God it is a Divine vision.

Thought is of the past and future; when it is emancipated from these two, the difficulty is solved.

MM II 175-177

The preacher is searing me with the heat of barren thought —
Where is the Saqi to throw water on my fire?!

Ḥāfeẓ

PONDERING *(tadabbor)*

Pondering signifies contemplation of the outcome of things, being close to consideration. The difference is that the latter involves the heart's activity with attention to proving things and the former, involves the heart's activity with attention to their outcome.

TJ

Conceptualization is pondering;
For those of intellect it is consideration.

Shabestari

SAGACITY AND SHREWDNESS *(feṭnat wa kiāsat)*

Sagacity involves the maintenance of moment, while shrewdness has to do with the perception of moment.

In the first instance, the word 'moment', refers to the particular state enjoyed by the wayfarer in actuality, while in the second, it signifies state in the overall or absolute sense. This is to say that the truly astute person is one who can maintain and preserve his state by observing the etiquette and conditions thereof, while one who recognizes states in general is yet more astute. Hence, sagacity is more specific than shrewdness, for it involves the maintaining of a particular state, while the latter involves perceiving states altogether.

TKQ 655

Since you have no sagacity nor the light of Divine guidance, continue to polish your face for the sake of the blind!

MM II 3223

I became aware of every plane
And perceived the mysteries due to sagacity.

MT 39

If he travels the way of meanness, he will consider
Miserliness to be reason and shrewdness.

HAu

HEART-DISCERNMENT *(ferāsat)*

In the terminology of the adepts of Reality, heart-discernment signifies visionary disclosure of certitude and direct observation of the Unseen.

TJ

Heart-discernment involves the emergence of hidden things, and the expulsion of darkness from the heart through the lights of contemplative vision.

TKQ 372

In the early stages, heart-discernment involves incoming thoughts *(khāṭer)* established in the heart and stations made sincere by the power of faith. In the final stages, it involves contemplative vision of the Unseen of the Unseen through the eyes of the Beloved.

RSh IV 178

The believer's divining is through heart-discernment --
Beyond our calendars and astrological tables.

Awḥadi

See heart-discernment as a Divine Attribute, not vain conjecture; the light of the heart has found light in the Universal Tablet.

MM VI 2744

His justice and equity have been perfected with God's seal;
His heart-discernment has superceded his disposition.

MT 24

When Yusof ebn Ḥosain was asked about the Prophetic Tradition, "Beware the believer's heart-discernment, for he sees with God's light,"[1], he replied, "This saying of the Prophet concerning the believer has to do with the grace granted one whose heart has been illuminated by God and whose breast has opened. This grace does not come to just anyone, however great his rectitude or however small his error. How could one who cannot decree the reality of faith, friendship with God and bliss for his *nafs*, decree God's grace for his *nafs?* The Prophet's statement about heart-discernment has to do with its being a grace for the believer without reference to any particular person."

LT 226

Heart-discernment involves the acquisition of insight of the spirit through knowledge of the Unseen.

SS 634

Literally, the word, *ferāsat,* denotes understanding through signs

---

1. See the author's *Traditions of the Prophet,* New York 1980, Vol. I, pp. 72-73.

and indications, or intuitive knowledge. In the terminology of the Path, as heart-discernment, it connotes awareness through the visionary disclosure of certitude and direct observation on the part of the inner consciousness. It has been said that heart-discernment involves God's awareness of the heart, which thereby becomes conscious of unseen things through God's light, which is that of the believer's heart, to which the Prophet was referring when he said that the "believer sees with God's light."[1]

The *Baḥr al-jawāher* (Sea of Jewels) states that the word, *ferāsat,* denotes astuteness, in the sense of a sudden arrival of understanding through something intangible. It has also been said that heart-discernment is the proof of hidden things through apparent things.

KF II 1123

Heart-discernment is an incoming thought that enters the hearts of people, rejecting whatever is opposed to the heart, which it takes over. Desires of the *nafs* do not fall within the scope of heart-discernment, which is based on the strength of one's faith. The stronger one's faith, the sharper one's heart-discernment.

RQ 366

Abu Sa'id Kharrāz said, "Whoever looks at God's light with the light of heart-discernment is seen by Him; the substance of his knowledge is from God, and he never wavers in remembrance. God's decree is always on this devotee's tongue, and whatever he says is through God's light, that is, the light which God has designated for him in particular."

RQ 367

It has been said that as soon as heart-discernment is fully realized, one attains the station of witnessing.

RQ 386

Abu Bakr Kattāni said, "Heart-discernment involves the attainment of certitude and the beholding of the Unseen, being due to faith and witnessing."

RQ 368[2]

---

1. *Ibid,*

Abu Bakr Wāseṭi said, "Heart-discernment is the illumination that glows in the heart and the gnosis that comes about in the inner consciousness *(serr)*, carrying it from one level of the Unseen to another, so that the devotee may see what God displays before him in order that he may speak from the depths of his being."

RQ 367[1]

Whoever can recognize the difference between inspiration and temptation and distinguish spiritual communication from worldly motivation possesses heart-discernment.

TKQ 365

The establishment of right opinion lies in heart-discernment. If a person's opinion is accompanied by heart-discernment, it comes to conform with Reality, becoming what is called right opinion.

TKQ 369

The reality of heart-discernment is soundness of heart, where one is immune from the infection of doubt. By means of heart-discernment, veracious incoming thoughts and infusions of the heart are distinguished in general.

Heart-discernment involves incoming thoughts that may be from either the attributes of the Majesty or those of Perfection, manifesting in a person's heart, so that one may approach perfection. The individual wayfarer is made ready by Majestic incoming thoughts and aided by Beautiful ones, and becomes established in attributes of perfection. Now, when one has mastered all these, one becomes stabilized.

Heart-discernment involves revelation of the mysteries of the realm of the Unseen through the visible realm. It is accompanied by the shedding of illusion and imagination on the part of the inner consciousness in the core of a heart at the station of visionary revelation and direct vision.

TKQ 890

---

2. TA 568.
1. TA 747.

DIVINE AND NATURAL HEART-DISCERNMENT *(ferāsat-e elāhiya wa ṭabiya)*

The result of perception in one who possesses Divine heart-discernment involves knowledge of Divine Unity and the Uniqueness *(waḥdāniyat)* and gnosis of Singularity and detachment from self *(tafrid)*. According to the Koran: "All things perish but His face," (XXVIII: 88), where His face with respect to a thing is the essential nature of that thing.

Now, heart-discernment may be either natural or spiritual. The spiritual is Divine heart-discernment, where theopany of Divine light is perceived directly through the insight of the believer. By this light he sees whatever is occurring within the object of his perception. Such perception may indicate a positive or negative outcome. Each act performed by a person may be good or bad before God regardless of whether this occurs in the presence of a heart-discerning person or not.

On the other hand, natural heart-discernment involves knowledge of praiseworthy and blameworthy dispositions and awareness of all physical acts, whether perceptible to the senses or not. It also involves distinguishing the sound nature from the unsound. The Perfect Human possesses both Divine and natural heart-discernment.

RSh II 422

THE DIFFERENCE BETWEEN HEART-DISCERNMENT AND OPINION *(farq miān-e ferāsat wa ḍhann)*

Abu 'Othmān Ḥiri said, "Heart-discernment is an opinion that conforms with God's view, whereas personal opinion may be either erroneous or correct. Now, when a believer becomes strengthened, becomes realized in heart-discernment, he conforms with God in his judgments, becoming of right opinion, for in this state he judges not by his own light, but by that of God."

TSS 163

THE DIFFERENCE BETWEEN HEART-DISCERNMENT AND INSPIRATION *(farq miān-e ferāsat wa elhām)*

Heart-discernment is the knowledge that is revealed from the Unseen through the scrutiny of outward indications. It is something that is common to the elect among the believers. The difference between heart-discernment and inspiration is that the former involves revelation of unseen things by way of the scrutiny of outward indications, while the latter has no intermediary.

MH 79

INTUITION *(tawwasom)*

"Indeed, therein are signs for those who have intuition." (XV: 75)

Intuition means having heart-discernment *(ferāsat),* which involves intimacy of what is unseen without either induction from what is seen nor deduction on the basis of experience. Intuition has three degrees:

1) That which is unexpected and rare, uttered by an unaware person once in a lifetime, because a sincere disciple must hear it without the utterer understanding of it or being conscious from whence it comes. It is the kind of thing which cannot be learned from a diviner or anyone of that nature, for such perception neither infers from insight nor springs from knowledge nor derives from experience.

2) That which is plucked from the tree of faith, appearing when faith is truly established, and shining with the light of visionary revelation.

3) That of the inner consciousness, which has no visible aspect, nor is it expressed vocally by the elect, either directly or by inspiration.

MS

Whenever the visionary gnostic attains contemplative vision of God in his heart, two lamps appear in his heart: one belonging to the intellect connected to the angelic domain and the other belonging to Divine faith. With the light of faith he perceives, in the Unseen, that of which God has informed us concerning heaven and what lies therein, as well as the Throne, the Pedestal and the expanses of the upper realm, along with the travelers within the Divine presence, the intimate angels and the spirits. By the lamp of the intellect he sees all that is found in the realm of dominion *(molk)* and that which is visible, coming to be able to read people's minds. In describing the insight of the heart of the gnostic and the appearance of the decrees of the Wrath and the Grace displayed before the eyes of the gnostic's intellect, the Koran states, "Indeed, there are signs for those who have intution." (XV: 75)

The Prophet said, "Beware of the heart-discernment of the believer, for he sees with the light of God."[1] In defining those who have intuition, some have said it is those who view incoming thoughts.

The gnostic said, "Intuition involves seeing the smile *(tabassom)* of the dawn of the Unseen, without obstruction and free of doubt."

MA 171

INSIGHT *(baṣirat)*

Insight is the faculty that glows in the heart with the light of Sanctity, whereby the realities and inner aspects of things are seen. It is for the heart what the inner eye is for the *nafs*, seeing the forms, the outer aspects, of things. The philosophers call insight the faculty of intellectual speculation *(qowwa-ye 'āqeliya-ye naẓariya).* When it becomes illumined with the light of the sanctity of God's Uniqueness *(waḥdāniyat),* the veils of conjecture and imagination are lifted from before the eye of insight. The resulting condition is called by the philosopher the faculty of sanctification *(qowwa-ye qodosiya).*

May the Lord grant that you gain such a heart,
That your heart may enjoy constant fulfillment.

RSh IV 17 [2]

If you must keep on looking at Me, then behold Me
With the eye of insight, like those who are aware.

Nāṣer Khosrau

Where is that person who can equal my insight, and become a true vicegerent.

MM IV 3359

Be silent, for it's question
And answer that plague insight.

Rumi

In the early stages, insight involves perception of the reality of the decrees of the Shari'at and the veracity of the communicator, while in the final stages it involves visionary revelation *(shohud)* of

1. *Ibid.*
2. ES 37.

multiplicity in Unity and total commitment to observe the requirements of servanthood and Lordship.

RSh IV 177

According to the Koran: "Say: This is my Way; I call to God with insight, I and whoever follows me."(XII: 108)

Insight is that which delivers one from perplexity, being of three degrees:

1) Knowing that God's Word, which prepares the way for establishment of the Shari'at, comes from a source the consequences of which one should not fear. Rather, one should see the rightness of it, so that one may, with certitude, draw benefit from the pleasure of it and, with a sense of protectiveness *(ghairat),* endure wrath in the way of supporting it.

2) Seeing justice as the purpose in God's guidance of someone or leading of someone astray, perceiving the working of God's kindness in the diversity of apportionment meted out to human beings, and regarding God's attraction as the cord of Union.

3) Insight that creates gnosis, affirms allusion *(eshārat),* and fosters the development of heart-discernment.

MS

The Twentieth Field is that of Insight, which derives from that of Certitude. According to the Koran: "They recollect, and lo! they have insight!" (VII: 201) Insight means seeing inwardly and involves three things:

That of acceptance, which involves attainment of the finding of acquaintanceship *(āshnā'i):* "Flashes of insight have come to you from your Lord." (VI: 104)

That of adherence, which involves firm commitment to the way of the Custom *sonna:* "I call to God with insight, I and whoever follows me." (XII: 108)

That of Reality, which involves seeing one's Lord with the eye of the heart: "A vision and a reminder for every contrite devotee." (L: 8)

The insight of acceptance is with reference to experiences, signs and proofs. That of adherence is through the Book, the *sonna* and what those who have gone before have handed down. That of Reality is a lamp in the heart, asking, "Where are you?", to which a voice in the ear replies, "I am here!", stating, "I am with You!"

SM

When the insight of the inner consciousness of the advanced one is opened with the key of the light of the Unseen, he looks thereby upon the wonders of the angelic realm and the rare expressions of the lights of the realm of ordainment and comes to understand the obscurities of the religious sciences, being guided by God to God's Way, with which he was pleased in pre-eternity *(azal)*. According to the Koran: "I call to God with insight, I and whoever follows me." (XII: 108)

The gnostic said, "Insight is the application of the collyrium of certitude with the brush of purity, taken from the collyrium-box of Reality, and applied to the eye of the spirit-at-peace."

MA 38

The Seventy-second Field is that of Insight, *(baṣar/baṣirat)*- which derives from that of Knowledge. The Koran tells how God "granted you hearing and sight." (XVI: 78; XXXII: 9; and LXVII: 23)

Insight is that which permits vision, being of three kinds:

1) That of the intellect, which has three benefits: a) recognizing what is to one's advantage and to one's detriment [spiritually], and paying heed to what will happen to one, for this will provide deliverance from blame; b) seeing the different levels of people, the tolerance of each according to his temperament, the power of each in wisdom, and the return of each according to his resolve; this brings about health; c) seeing what is the best for each thing in every matter, at every moment and with every person; this is the raiment of magnanimity. All these are the measures of the intellect. All else is tribulation.

2) That of wisdom, which has three indications: a) seeing kindness at every opportunity, so that resistance may be dispelled; b) being astonished at whatever occurs, so that haste may be dispelled; and c) being aware of God's intimations in all God's works, so that acquaintanceship may be forged. The joy of this Way is intimacy [with God].

3) That of heart-discernment *(ferāsat)*, which is of three kinds: a) that which is due to experience, which is for all who discern; b) that which is based on reasoning, which is for all who possess intellect; and c) that of heart-regard *(naẓar-e del)*, which is through that

light which believers have in the heart.

The heart-discernment due to experience comes through what one has seen, through what one has heard, or through wisdom. That based on reasoning formed according to the rule of the ßhari'at in matters of religion, through intelectual conjecture in non-religious instances, and by the rule of nature in which ordinary people engage. That of visionary heart-discernment comes through lightning, a true flash in the heart, or turbulence that arises in the depths of being, leading to Reality, or through the decisive comprehension of a decree directly from the Unseen, and is special to Kheḍhr.

SM

Each sight has an insight;
Each insight has an effect.

Khāju-ye Kermāni

Spiritual Organs

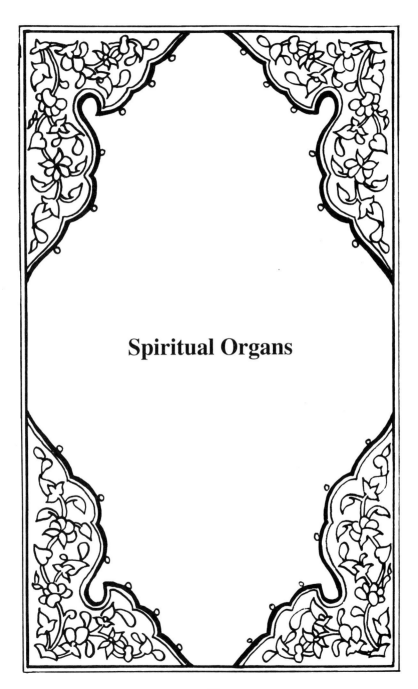

THE INTELLECT *('aql)*

The intellect is a substance distinct from matter, with which it interacts. It may be defined as the rational soul *(nafs-e nāṭeqa)*, or ego, the 'I' to which each individual refers.

The intellect has been variously described as a Divinely created spiritual substance, attached to the body; a light in the heart, distinguishing Truth from untruth; an incorporeal substance linked to the body in order to control it. Unlike this former definition, it can also be a faculty of the rational soul, for which it is clear that the intellectual faculty serves as the instrument to apply reason, as a knife is used for cutting.

There are those who maintain that the intellect, the *nafs* and the mind are one and the same thing, which is termed, intellect, when its role of perceiver is considered, *nafs* in the capacity of its power to control, and mind in its aptitude for perceiving.

It has been maintained, further, that the intellect is that by which the realities of things are judged, or, again, that it is located in the mind or according to others, in the heart.

TJ

What do you know of the sage's view of the intellect?
It borrows a light from the lamp of the Eternal,
So that it may reveal clearly to the nafs
Those spiritual realities which shine on it.

NP

God's fire singed the feathers of the Intellect,
Out of jealous protectiveness of His domain.
The intellect, like us, is bewildered;
Like us, it is confounded by God's Essence.

HH 61

How much nonsense must one take from this intellect?
How long must one still be colored by this world and nature?

HH 62

The intellect is neither a means nor a cause for gaining gnosis of God; rather, it is a means of observing servanthood, because it is a discriminator, and discrimination requires two things, while God is one alone, where the intellect has no access. When one acquires an intellect, one cannot know God as He is unless He Himself decrees.

KST 164

Out of all created beings God designated man to receive the lights of the intellect, so that he might achieve worship of God in every state, for the intellect is the medium of servanthood, while gnosis is the medium of Lordship. The intellect is guided by rules, while gnosis is guided by signs. Through the light of the intellect the Truth may be distinguished from untruth. The intellect is the minister governing the spirit and the treasurer of ones being. It is the scribe of revelation and inspiration. It is the copyist of the register of the Divine message. The intellect inculcates of ethics and determines practices. It is the restrainer from temptation and the cleanser of filth, the merchant of the caravan of the heart, and the chief of those involved in the world. the intellect refines the senses and kneads the confection of spiritual practice. It is the trusted lieutenant of the Law-giver and the chamberlain of the court of Glory.

If the intellect did not exist, there would be no scion of Adam's clay in the dominion of the heart to observe servanthood. It comes directly from God to regulate God's marketplace. It is the designer of the workshop of the angelic realm, using whatever comes from God to appropriate the imagination and compel it to produce designs under its authority.

RQR 71

The intellect is the instrument of discrimination between good and evil, virtue and vice.

EE

It was God's wisdom that gave the moth to the intellect,
That it might light the darkness of error with the candle of guidance.

Kamāl Khojandi

When a dervish asked the master [Abu Sa'id Abe'l-Khair] the meaning of intellect, he replied, "It is the instrument of servanthood. One cannot discover the mysteries of Lordship with it, for it is transitory, and the transitory has no access to the Eternal."

AT 315

Since the intellect is a knocker on the outside
Of the door, it has no news of God's Attributes.

Sanā'i

If you block the intellect, we are not frightened;
Bring wine, for that baggage has no role in our province.

Ḥāfeẓ

Although the intellect is the noblest of created things, the rank of the spirit is higher, for the spirit belongs to the realm of the Divine Command *(amr)*, not that of creation, where the intellect reigns supreme.

Three Prophetic Traditions on this subject mean the same: "The first thing that God created was the intellect," "The first thing that God created was my [Moḥammad's] light," and "The first thing that God created was the Pen," for the Prophet was the site of manifestation, in the visible world, of the form of the relative spirit in the Unseen. The First Intellect was a light emanating from the relative spirit, and the Pen, which signifies the First Intellect, was the medium for expressing the forms of Divine words and the intermediary to bring them out of the site of Concentration *(jam')* onto the level of differentiation *(tafṣil)*.

MH 102

The intellect is the guide of servanthood, guiding the wayfarer to the reality of patience and fortitude. Now, anyone who seeks to attain the object of his worship, by means of the intellect worships the intellect itself, not God.

TKQ 377

Now courageously restore yourself, to that disposition; take the intellect which contemplates patience as your guide.

MM VI 3977

The intellect guides one ultimately to bewilderment, and the ultimate end of bewilderment is intoxication.

TKQ 378

When Nuri was asked, "What is the guide to God?", he replied, "God." "Then what is the role of the intellect?" they asked. "The intellect is impotent," he replied, "and that which is impotent can show the way only to that which is impotent like itself."

KST 155

Being escorted by the intellect, we got nowhere;
Our guide had more twists and turns than the way!
Ṣā'eb Tabrizi

Having no one else to travel with, I went with the intellect.
As we journeyed to the next lane, the skirts of my robe
Were torn to pieces by the thorns of his arguments.
Sā'eb Tabrizi

In his *Mathnawi* Rumi has used the intellect to represent variously the Prophet and the Pole *(qoṭb),* with the implications of the worldly intellect *('aql-e ma'āsh)* and the other-worldly intellect *('aql-e ma'ād).*

a) Representing the Prophet:

As Moses stepped on the Path of annihilation Pharaoh asked, "Who are you?"

He replied, "I am the Intellect, the messenger of the Almighty; I am the proof of God; I am the protection against error."

MM IV 2309

b) As the Pole:

As far as you can, endeavor to satisfy the Pole, so that he may gain strength and hunt the wild beasts. When he is ailing, the people remain hungry, for all food provided for the gullet comes from the hand of the intellect.

MM V 2340-2341

c) As the worldly intellect:

When a man's intellect has been his teacher, thenceforth the intellect becomes his pupil.

MM I 1065

d) As the other-worldly intellect:

The intellect says, like Gabriel, "O Aḥmad [Moḥammad], if I

take one more step, it will burn me. You must leave me; henceforth, advance alone; this is my limit, O sultan of the soul!"

MM I 1066-1067

Rumi has, in another context, represented the intellect as being the opposite of passion, which itself is brought about by illusion:

The intellect is the contrary of passion. Brave man, do not call intellect that which is attached to passion. That which is a beggar of passion — call it illusion; illusion is the counterfeit of the pure gold of the intellectual faculties.

Without a touchstone, illusion and intellect are not clearly distinguished; quickly bring both to the touchstone!

MM IV 2301-2303

VISION OF THE INTELLECT *(ro'yat-e 'aql)*

When, in the course of [the spirit's] circling on the wings of reflection *(fekr)* on God's signs, the lights of the Attributes appear to it in the Majesty of the signs. A Sufi master has stated, "I have never looked upon anything without seeing God therein." According to the Koran: "Indeed, herein are signs for those of intellect." (XX: 54 & 128)

The gnostic said, "When the lover's intellect is purified of the turbidites of materiality, he sees God in every beautiful guise, this being one of the levels of disguise *(eltebās)*."

MA 126

GNOSIS OF THE INTELLECT *(ma'refat-e 'aql)*

The intellect is one of the elect Dominical lights of God, Who plants it in a person's heart, whereby one may distinguish truth from untruth. In itself it is a substance connected with Sanctity, whereby the quiddity of the realities of things may be perceived. The Koran speaks of those having "hearts wherewith they do not understand." (VII: 179)

The Prophet stated, "Most of the people of paradise are simple, while those of the empyrean realms *('elliyin)* are wise." A gnostic has said, "The intellect is the instrument of servanthood; it is not for contemplating the Lordship."

The gnostic said, "The intellect is the eye with which the spirit looks upon the angelic realm *(malakut)*, whereby it knows the realities of the affairs of the world and the hereafter."

MA 153

THE ACTIVE INTELLECT *('aql-e fa'āl)*

The philosophers call the Tenth Intellect [in a cosmological hierarchy of successive emanations from Necessary Being *(wājeb al-wojud)]* the Active Intellect, known to the theologians as Gabriel or the Holy Spirit. It is the lowest of the Intellects, being called the Active Intellect because it produces human souls, activating them from potential to actual existence.

***

Clip the wings of your active intellect;
Then make your nafs subject to your intellect.

M

What is the diver?
The Active Intellect,
Worthy to be a prophet's intellect.

Sanā'i

THE SAVOURING INTELLECT *('aql-e dhauqi)*

The savouring intellect is said to result from the savouring *(dhauq)* and imbibing *(shorb)* of the wine *(sharāb)* of love *('eshq)* and loving-kindness *(maḥabbat)*. It may also be called the bestowing intellect *('aql-e mauhebati)*.

***

If you do not acquire the savouring intellect,
How can you attain the realities?

M

THE SECOND INTELLECT *('aql-e thani)*

Whilst the Holy Spirit is known as the First Intellect because of its illumination, the Second Intellect is known as the Universal Soul because of its darkness.

The First Intellect calls you to God;
The Second Intellect drags you away from Him.

RSh I 287

THE PARTICULAR OR INDIVIDUAL INTELLECT *('aql-e jozwi yā 'aql-e fardi)*

The particular, or individual, intellect is said to be that of the philosophers and the exoteric theologians.

***

The particular intellect is not the intellect capable of production; it is only the receiver of technique and is needy.

MM IV 1295

The particular intellect denies love while appearing to be its confidant.

MM I 1295

The apprehensive faculty *(wahm)* and opinion *(ẓann)* are the bane of the particular intellect, because its dwelling-place is in darkness.

MM I 1558

Do not take the particular intellect as your vizier; make the Universal Intellect your vizier, O king.

MM IV 1258

The particular intellect has given the intellect a bad name.
Worldly desire has driven man helpless.

MM V 463

THE CROSS-EYED INTELLECT *('aql-e kāzh yā 'aql-e luch)*

Rumi uses the term cross-eyed intellect to symbolize dualism (literally, seeing double).

***

That malign wretch was babbling silly nonsense about the master; the cross-eyed man is always of cross-eyed intellect.

MM II 3398

THE INTELLECT OF FAITH *('aql-e imāni)*

In Sufi terminology, the intellect of faith is the faculty which restrains one from desires of the *nafs* and their harmful consequences:

The intellect that is allied to faith is like a just police inspector. It is the guardian and magistrate of the city of the heart. It is mentally alert like a cat; the thief remains in the hole, like a mouse.

The intellect in the body is the magistrate of faith, through fear of whom the *nafs* is confined.

MM IV 1086-1987

THE PRACTICAL INTELLECT
('aql-e mostafād yā 'aql-e be'l-mostafād)

The practical intellect is one which retains the images that it perceives.

TJ

When the material intellect *('aql-e hayulāni)* becomes actualized out of its state of potentiality, it is termed the practical intellect.

D

If being is not utilized, it becomes corrupt;
When intellect is utilized, it is practical.

HH

THE MULTIPEL INTELLECT *('aql-e moḍhā'ef)*

The practical intellect is called the multiple intellect in the sense that, on the one hand, it draws emanating grace *(faiḍh)* from what is above it, namely, the Active Intellect *('aql-e fa''āl)* and, on the other, the material intellect *('aql-e hayulāni),* the intellect-in-aptitude *('aql-e be'l-malaka),* the intellect-in-practice *('aql-e be'l-fe'l),* and the outer and inner senses.

***

THE MATERIAL INTELLECT *('aql-e hayulāni)*

The material intellect represents the unrealized aptitude for the perception of intelligible things, being purely potential, disassociated from any application, as in the case of infants. It is identified with matter *(hayulā)* in the sense that the *nafs* at this stage is like primal matter in that within the limits of its essence it is free of the impression of forms.

TJ

THE CONGENITAL INTELLECT *('aql-e mādar-zād)*

The congenital intellect is a part of one's nature. The Sufis believe that each person is born with a different intellect, in contrast to the Mu'tazilites[1],basic to his individual nature. This why each individual sees Reality from a different point of view.

The Sufis maintain that it is through the Path of Love and loving-kindness that subjective differentiation disappears. It is by ceasing to adhere to one's intellect and taking up the Path of Love that one may be delivered from the bonds of subjectively differentiating things and come to see all things as One Being.

***

THE BASE INTELLECT *('aql-e past)*

The base intellect is another name for the worldly intellect *('aql-e ma'āsh)*.

***

This base intellect has the same temperament as the ass, its only thought is how it shall get hold of fodder *('alaf)*.

MM II 1858

THE ACQUIRED INTELLECT *('aql-e taḥsili yā 'aql-e ektesābi)*

The acquired intellect is one that is obtained through experience and the acquisition of knowledge.

***

The acquired intellect is like a series of conduits that run into a house from the streets; if the house's waterway is blocked, it is without any supply of water. It remains parched and miserable and with a hundred afflictions.

MM IV 1967-1968

THE SWERVING OR CROW INTELLECT *('aql-e zāgh)*

The swerving or crow intellect is what Rumi calls the worldly *('aql-e ma'āsh)*, bodily *('aql-e jesmāni)* or sensual intellect *('aql-e shahwāni)*:

The Universal Intellect *('aql-e koll)*, the eye of which does "not swerve", is the light of the elect; the swerving or crow intellect is the

1. Proponants of Kalām or dogmatic theology.

grave-master for the spiritually dead.

MM IV 1310

THE ULTIMATE INTELLECT *('aql-e 'aql)*

Rumi calls the friend of God *(wali)* the ultimate intellect:

The friends of God are the ultimate intellect, and all intellects from the beginning to the end are under their control, like camels [under their riders].

MM I 2498

The philosopher is in bondage to things perceived by the intellect, but the princely rider, the ultimate intellect, turned out to be the pure friend of God.

MM IV 2527

THE GUIDING AND THE WORLDLY INTELLECT *('aql-e hedāyat wa 'aql-e ma'āsh)*

In itself, the intellect is one entity, though possessing two aspects. One in respect to the Creator and may be called the guiding intellect, being exclusive to believers. The other is in respect to the creation and may be called the worldly intellect, being common to all.

For those of faith and seekers of God and the hereafter, the worldly intellect is subservient to the guiding intellect. They consider the former to be valid where it conforms to and is consistent with the latter, and follows its strictures. However, if the worldly intellect should oppose the guiding intelect, they consider it to have slipped from the rank of validity and do not heed it. For this reason, worldly people accuse them of weakness of intellect, unaware that they have an intellect higher than that of the worldly ones.

MH 56

THE OTHER-WORLDLY, THE WORLDLY AND THE PARTICULAR INTELLECT *('aql-e ma'ād, 'aql-e ma'āsh wa 'aql-e jozwi)*

Love is ascribed to the inner aspect, the reality, of the intellect. One must be aware that the spirit has two aspects:

One directed towards the realm of Unity and the region of Sanctity: From this point of view, the spirit is called love. Sometimes the term love simply relates to the attention and attraction of the spirit towards Unity.

One directed towards the realm of multiplicity, for the sake of expansion of knowledge of phenomena. This aspect has, in turn, two manifestations: a) perception of universal truths and sacred realities *(ma'nā)*, known as the other-worldly intellect, and b) perception of individual states, physical actions, and material entities, known as the worldly or particular intellect, which is in contradistinction to love.

TT 216

THE INSTINCTUAL, THE INSPIRATIONAL, THE FIGURATIVE AND THE TRUE INTELLECT
('aql-e gharizi, 'aql-e elhāmi. 'aql-e majāzi wa 'aql-e ḥaqiqi)

The instinctual intellect consists of knowledge that God has caused to appear in man's nature, whereby he may distinguish between blameworthy and praiseworthy acts. It is this trait that distinuishes man from other creatures. It is a positive quality, because through it appear actions which are in themselves important in the corporeal realm, strengthening one in spiritual practice. This instinctual intellect is located in the brain, as a part of man's physical form, although it steals from the realm of the heart, taking divine knowledge therefrom. Moreover, it experiences increase and decrease, because it is not in itself independent. Since instinctual intellect is not perfect, it brings disorder to the realm of natural occurrences.

The inspirational intellect represents angelic communication, which comes to people every instant. Through these Acts of God it is aware of the acts of created beings, and correspondingly, it knows the works and decrees of God. Its consciousness moves back and forth, powered by the light in God's signs. The inspirational intellect brings increase in one's state through God's emanating grace *(faiḍh)* and separates the transitory from the Eternal. It brings onslaughts of Divine love and wrath from the plane of the angelic realm. It refines the individual's inner consciousness, serves the individual's stations, and pleads for states on the individual's behalf.

The inspirational intellect is located in the pearl-generating inner being of one whose angelic sagacity *(feṭnat)* makes him spiritually well-versed and knowledgable. If he did not have knowledge of the heart, the demons would disturb him, and his soul would not have come to terms with the Koran, the custom *(sonnat)* and the Shari'at. He is in harmony with Reality, in adhering to the Shari'at. Elect knowledge is clear to him. He knows the forms hidden in infusions of wrath and grace, so that his heart is unerring in experiencing visionary disclosure *(mokāshafa)*.

The figurative intellect is a perception which God has created in the form of the heart, such that it is not constant in every state, because the heart is turned about by God's Will. Sometimes it is disengaged by blasts of Wrath and sometimes by breezes of Grace. It is because of its figurativeness that it is not lasting. When the figurative intellect is engaged, spiritual practice is assiduously observed, whereas when it is disengaged, one indulges oneself freely in what is prohibited. When God wishes to create ordainment in the world of humanity, He extinguishes light from the heart.

The True Intellect was created by God out of pure light before He created existence. He spoke to it and showed it the wonders of Lordship, so that it might be firm in servanthood. Once He had created things, He sent it into the corporeal realm, entrusting it to the Spirit. This intellect is located in the Sacred Spirit, with which it is so completely integrated that they cannot be known independently of one another. In fact the spirit's acquisition of the attributes of the True Intellect is the goal of created beings, where the objective is to become the vicegerent of earthly creatures, the recipient of God's words, the believer in God's wonders, the seat of heart-discernment, the winged bearer of visionary disclosure, and the witness of witnessing *(moshāhada)*.

It is the True intellect that, on the level of realities, conforms with states, being detached from the impurities of human nature and the turbulence of natural motivations, for it is a flower appearing in the clay of man, for man's rational spirit to smell and, through its aroma, become established in gnosis. It is this intellect that purchases the light of wisdom from the marketplace of the Eternal and puts an end to the ravages of the *nafs*. It is this intellect that remains with the everlasting spirit.

The True intellect abides immortally, for it dwells in immortality with God. It increases through the light of theophany. The more that is Divinely revealed, the greater the light of this intellect, although it never attains perfection because of its transitory nature, being still on the level of the devotee, whereas perfection is Divine. The True intellect is not, while God is.

Gnosis of the intellect is of three kinds:

1) Ordinary gnosis of intellects, which is no higher than the instinctual intellect

2) Elect gnosis of the inspirational intellect

3) Elect gnosis of the Universal Intellect (*'aql-e koll*), which is the True Intellect, which, with God's support, is God's vicegerent.

By the door of the Unseen stands the translator, Intellect;
The soul is the king of the body, and the Intellect king of the soul.

RQR 71

THE INTELLECTS (*'oqul yā kherad-hā*)

In the Mathnawi, Rumi employs the term, the Intellects, to refer to the Ten Intellects which the ancients held to emanate successively from Necessary Being, out of which emerged the First Intellect, from which derived the Second, along with the ninth heaven, and continuing on down to the Tenth Intellect and the first heaven; and from the Tenth Intellect emerged the realm of the elements and the three kingdoms of nature (animal, vegetable and mineral).

***

To the eye of the Prophet the treasuries of the celestial spheres and Intellects seemed worthless as a straw...

MM I 3955

THE INTELLECTUAL TRIANGLE (*mothallath-e 'aqli*)

The intellectual triangle represents the relationship between the intellect, comprehension (*fahm*) and heart-discernment (*ferāsat*): the intellect corresponding to the Divine Acts displayed in the derivatives of the various and diverse works of God; comprehension corresponding to theophanies of the Attributes of Lordship, displayed in the mirrors of the multifarious entities; and heart-discernment corresponding to a radiant flashing sparkle (*lom'a-ye bāreqa-ye shāreqa*) beyond the veils of the Unseen in the hearts of those who enjoy contemplative vision (*shohud*) from the Divine Uniqueness (*waḥdāniyat*).

The consequence of perception by the intellect is recognizing of God's Acts and gnosis of the created entities fashioned by God's decrees. The consequence of perception through comprehension is knowledge of God's Attributes and qualities on the level of the Divine plane. Finally, the consequence of possessing heart-discernment is knowledge of Divine Unity *(tauḥid)*, the Uniqueness, detachment from the world *(tafrid)*, and the Singularity *(fardāniyat)*, according to the Koranic passage: "All things perish except His face." (XXVIII: 88)

RSh II 287

THE FIRST INTELLECT *('aql-e awwal)*

The *Kashf al-loghāt (Glossary)* states that in the terminology of the Sufis, the First Intellect is the level of Unity. It states further that the First Intellect and the Universal Intellect are said to be the same as Gabriel. The *Farhang (Lexicon)* defines it as the Divine Throne, adding that it is said to represent the origin and reality of man in the sense that it serves as an emanating intermediary for the emergence of the Universal Soul, which is known by four other names: 1) the Universal Intellect, 2) the First Pen, 3) the Sublime Spirit, and 4) the Mother Book *(ommo' l-ketāb)*. From the point of view of Adam's reality, the form is the Universal Intellect, while Eve's form is the Universal Soul.

KF II 1030

The exoteric clergy consider the First Intellect to be the Sacred Spirit.

The First Intellect is the product of God's Attributes;
He has given it access through gnosis of Him.

HH 61

COMPARISON BETWEEN THE FIRST INTELLECT AND THE UNIVERSAL SOUL
(moqāyasa-ye 'aql-e awwal wa nafs-e koll)

The First Intellect embraces all the world, and the Universal Soul all the particulars thereof; it, in turn is embraced by the First Intellect, which represents the summation of all things, while the Universal Soul represents the differentiation of them.

The First Intellect is said to be the same as the Tablet of Ordainment, the Alabaster Pearl *(dorrato' l-baiḍhā')* and the Spiritual Adam; and the Universal Soul is said to be the same as the Guarded Tablet *(lauḥ-e maḥfuẓ)*, the Ruby *(yāquto' l-ḥamrā')* and the Spiritual Eve.

The Universal Soul is the elect manifestation of Mercy associated with Necessary Being, while the First Intellect is the common manifestation for all contingent being. The Universal Man embraces all the Divine Names, epitomized on the level of the Spirit and differentiated on that of the Sublime Name, which is the Heart.

The First Intellect and the Universal Soul are two books, epitomized and differentiated, which represent the form of the Mother Book, which is the plane of the Divine Knowledge.

The First Intellect is called the Mother Book by virtue of embracing all things in summation, while the Universal Soul represents the Manifest Book *(ketāb-e mobin)* by virtue of embracing all things in differentiation. Furthermore, the First Intellect is to the world as the human spirit is to the body, while the Universal Soul is to the world as the heart is to the limbs.

RSh II 257

THE UNIVERSAL INTELLECT *('aql-e koll)*

The Universal Intellect has traditionally been considered synonymous with the First Intellect.

***

The Sufis perceive the Universal Intellect to be the reality of the Moḥammadan light, the inner being of the Perfect Man, and the soul of friends of God:

The Universal Intellect wanders confounded by You;
All entities are subject to Your decree.

MM IV

The whole world is the form of the Universal Intellect, which is the father of whomsoever is a follower of the Divine word.

MM IV 3259

Concerning the Universal Intellect, God has said, "The eye did not turn aside," (LIII: 17), but the particular intellect *('aql-e jozwi)* is looking in every direction.

MM IV 1309

Similarly, the disciple full of egotism sees himself in the mirror of the Master's body. How should he see the Universal Intellect behind the mirror at the time of speech and discourse?

MM V 1437-1438

The Universal Intellect is a discourse from God's book;
The Universal Soul is but a footman by His gate.
HH 62

God's first sign was the Universal Intellect,
Which appeared in Him like the bā' *of* B'esme'llāh.
GR

THE DIFFERENCE BETWEEN THE FIRST, THE UNIVERSAL AND THE WORLDLY INTELLECT *('aql-e awwal wa 'aql-e koll wa 'aql-e ma'āsh)*

The First Intellect is the site where the Divine Knowledge takes shape in Being, for it is the sublime aspect of knowledge. Subsequently, this Knowledge descends onto the Guarded Tablet *(lauḥ-e maḥfuẓ),* of which it is the summation of all tablets, while the *lauḥ-e maḥfuẓ* is the differentiated aspect of it. In turn, the First Intellect is the differentiated aspect of the epitomized Divine Knowledge, which is revealed on the *lauḥ-e maḥfuẓ*.

The First Intellect is one of the Divine mysteries and cannot be contained by the *lauḥ-e maḥfuẓ* because it is only a part of the Divine Knowledge.

Further, the Divine Knowledge is the Mother Book *(ommo'l-ketāb),* while the First Intellect is the Manifest Imam and the *lauḥ-e maḥfuẓ* of the Manifest Book *(ketāb-e mobin).* The *lauḥ-e maḥfuẓ* follows the Divine Pen, to which it adheres. Being the First Intellect, the Pen has authority over the *lauḥ-e maḥfuẓ* and serves to differentiate the decrees epitomized in the ink well of the Divine Knowledge, from which it is translated into *nun* [the primordial ink or blackness which represents potential differentiated forms].

The First Intellect, the Universal Intellect and the worldly intellect differ from one another in the following manner:

The First Intellect is the first outward, created, determined form, emanating from the Divine Knowledge. It could also be described as the first differentiation of the Divine summation, as referred to in the Prophet's statement: "The first thing created by God was the Intellect." It is the nearest of the created realities to the Divine ones.

The Universal Intellect is the straight balance, being the scales of justice weighing and discriminating under the aegis of the Spirit. Briefly, the Universal Intellect is intellectual *('āqela),* that is to say, a luminous perceiver through which the forms of knowledge existing in the First Intellect are made apparent.

The worldly intellect is a light functioning according to the dictates of the law of reflection *(fekr)*, perceiving solely by means of reflection. Furthermore, the perception which it has is only an aspect of the Universal Intellect, for it has no access to the First Intellect, which is beyond limitation by reason or circumscription by the weighing of the scales. Rather, it is the site of the emanation of the sacred revelation to the *nafs*.

As the balance of justice is for the purpose of weighing and discriminating, the Universal Intellect is beyond the governance of all law but itself, while weighing everything according to a given standard. The worldly intellect has no more than a single standard, namely, reflection. As a balance, it has only a single scale, which is habit; a single side, which is outwardly apparent; and a single strength, which is that of material nature; in contrast to the Universal Intellect, which has two scales, namely, wisdom and power; two sides, namely, Divine dictates and natural potential; and two powers, namely, the Divine Will and the dictates of creation, which constitute multiple standards.

Hence, the Universal Intellect is the straight balance, which cannot deviate, nor be ever unjust; furthermore, nothing eludes it; in contrast to the worldly intellect, which is deviated from occasionally, and many things slip from it, because it has only one scale and one side.

Accordingly, the First Intellect can be compared to the sun, the Universal Intellect to water in which the sun's light is reflected, and the worldly intellect to a ray of light reflected from that water onto a wall.

Whoever looks at the water, grasps the nature of the sun correctly, seeing its light as it is, such that if he were to look directly at the sun, he would notice no significant difference between the two. The difference is that one must look up to see the sun, while one looks down at the water. By the same token, one who gains knowledge from the First Intellect looks upward by the light of his heart towards the Divine Knowledge, while one whose knowledge comes from the Universal Intellect looks downward by the light of his heart towards the site of the Book, learning what is to be known about phenomenal beings.

The Universal Intellect is the purview of discrimination of knowledge which God has imposed on the *lauḥ-e maḥfuẓ*, within which man may gain knowledge, whether through the dictates of wisdom or by the standards of power, whether rationally or otherwise. Its search for knowledge involves descent, which is one of the intrinsic universal characteristics of created being. In its discrimination it is seldom in error, except with respect to things that God has designated to be known only by Himself. This is in contrast to the First Intellect, which receives this knowledge directly from God.

KF 1028)

THE INTELLECT AND LOVE *('aql wa 'eshq)*

The Sufis believe that the intellect derives from the senses and subjective perceptions. Since these are limited and deficient, the intellect, too, being their product, must be likewise. Accordingly, the intellect cannot perceive Reality, which is universal and infinite. In contrast, love is Divine and is of the substance of universal spiritual realities *(ma'nā),* having been entrusted to the heart from the realm of the Infinite. Hence, it is acquainted with Reality and may effectively lead the Sufi to the level of perfection.

The question arises here as to what role the intellect plays in the life of the Sufi. Our answer is that for the non-Sufi the heart is subservient to the intellect whereas for the Sufi the intellect is the sincere servant of the heart. It should be noted that the intellect which the Sufis contrast to love is the practical intellect *('aql-e jozwi).*

***

When the light of the of the sun of love appears, burning all that is other than the Beloved with its rays of jealousy, the light of the intellect is overwhelmed. As the Sultan of love dominates the lover's being, He slaughters all other than the Beloved with the sword of jealousy.

RSh I 209

The eye of the intellect is concealed from the perception of the reality of love. The intellect is incapable of seeing the light of love, for love is at a level beyond that of the intellect, which consequently, lacks the power of perceiving it. Love is a pearl hidden in the oystershell of the soul, that has plunged into the depths of the sea of ordainment, on the shores of which the intellect has stopped, prevented from going further by fear of hidden afflictions from the Eternal.

L 98

The plane of love is far higher than the court of the intellect.
Its threshold is kissed by the one who carries his soul in his sleeve.

Ḥāfeẓ

What is love? An ocean emerging from a drop
That turns intellect into the sole of the shoe of aspiration.

MN 41

Intellect: "I am the one who causes perfections."
Love: "I am not bound by imagination."
Intellect: "I am an all-embracing, developed metropolis."
Love: "I am a crazy and intoxicated moth."
Intellect: "I quench the flame of affliction."
Love: "I drink the drought of annihilation."
Intellect: "I am the Joanna of the garden of health."
Love: "I am the Joseph of the prison of blame."
Intellect" "I'm an aware Alexander."
Love: "I am an elect *qalandar.*"[1]
Intellect: "I am supreme in the city of being."
Love: "I'm better than the existence of being."
Intellect: "I'm a dealer in the silver of characteristics."
Love: "I'm an intimate of the sanctum of Union."
Intellect: "I piously go about my business."
Love: "I have no business with claims."
Intellect: "I'm a teacher of the school of knowledge."
Love: "I'm the fragrance of the musk-bag of submission."
Intellect: "I'm the mirror of the excellence of all who attain it."
Love: "I'm beyond all matter of loss or gain."
Intellect: "I remember all subtleties and marvels."
Love: "I am conscious only of Him."
Intellect: "I'm engaged with resolve in spiritual practice."
Love: "I sit at the threshold of His presence."
Intellect: "I am concealed by the refined ones."
Love: "The seasoned drinkers of dregs are mine."
Intellect: "Mine is the science of eloquence."
Love: "Mine is deliverance from both the worlds."
Intellect: "I'm the arbiter of the Law."

---

1. A detached dervish of a rapturous state see Vol. VI, pp. 123-124.

Love: "I'm the seeker of the Path."
Intellect: "I'm a person's monitor."
Love: "I'm the paragon of excellence."
Intellect: "I open the door of comprehension."
Love: "I scour off the rust of illusion."
Intellect: "I am tied to duties."
Love: "I am fit for honors."
Intellect: "I am the saying and doing of the intelligent. How dare you open your mouth to slander me? Who are you? Your being has been burnt up, while I am sincere in garments stitched with piety. You are a ray of trial and affliction, while I am the intermediary for the gaining of God's guidance."
Love: "I am crazed with a drought of savouring, I ignite the flame of yearning, the seed of the crop of affection. O Intellect, who are you? You're concerned with conduct on the Way, while I'm an intimate of the King. Hence, at that hour when market-day arrives, the New Year's Day of love for the Beloved, I'll be speaking to the Beloved, seeking the kernel without the shell. I'll neither address myself to the veil nor shall I be afraid of the veil. I shall enter drunkenly and be raised to the honor of nearness. I shall don the crown of acceptance and throw you, Intellect, out forthwith!"

Suddenly, in the midst of their exchange, the messenger of awakening arrived from the Way, bearing a letter addressed to Love from the King, sealed with lovers' sighs. This was a decree, declaring: "O Intellect! Human nature is your garb, comprehension your loincloth. Be content with your ministerial rank. Though you enjoy reputation, you have no real mettle. If you're threatened with attack, into a hole you scuttle. The very moment you see that the attacker is bold, you become frail; you're confused and don't know what to do. When agitation throws the town into an uproar or spite rocks the foundations of the breast, you won't be willing to take a risk and snatch the blade from the enemy's hand. In the city of the body, a brave king and obeyed ruler must be wise, such that if he sees a pen, he becomes a line, or when a storm appears, he becomes a duck, or when earthquake threatens, he doesn't fall to pieces. Brave king, submissive subjects."

Now, it is Love who possesses these qualities and, hence, is king of the domain of the heart. Intellect, which is but a slave, how far can it travel? With a pothole at every step and its eyes in a veil, "indeed, this is an astounding thing!" (XXXVIII: 5)

So, one must be sincere, free of hypocrisy. One must have love as bright as a lightning flash, so that the inner consciousness may be set aglow with a flame and be inebriated with a drought, and we may be snatched from ourselves in a flash, in a twinkling, and through attraction join the Beloved!

Z 5

Intellect declares that three dimensions are the limit,
with no way beyond.

Love says that there is a way and says that it has traveled it many times.

Intellect saw the marketplace and began to trade;

Love perceived many further markets
beyond that one.

Intellect warned, "Don't take a step!
There are only thorns in annihilation!"

Love explained to Intellect,
"All those thorns are only in you!"

Rumi

In pre-eternity a ray of Your beauty
dawned in theophany;

Love appeared and set the whole
world afire.

Intellect wanted to light a lamp with that flame;
The lightning of jealousy flashed and threw the world into turmoil.

Ḥāfeẓ

With love, if you become non-existent,
you come into Existence;
With intellect, if you come to exist,
you become abject.

Now, note this curious thing:
It may happen that in drinking
The wine of love, you turn sober,
in order to become drunk!

L 113

THE *NAFS (nafs)*[1]

Nafs is the term that Sufis apply to the faculty that engenders self-centredness, attachment to the passions, and anger and aggressiveness in a person.

***

How can one attain Your lane,
when all one sees
Are deserts all around Your lane
because of one's nafs?

Sanā'i

The term *nafs* etymologically signifies the essence and reality of anything, but in popular language it has many contradictory connotations, such as spirit, manliness, body and blood. The realized ones of this group, however, are agreed that it is the source and foundation of evil, but while some assert that it is a substance located in the body, as the spirit is, others hold it to be an attribute of the body, as life is. However, all agree that through it base qualities are manifested and that it is the immediate cause of blameworthy actions.

Both the *nafs* and the spirit are subtleties existing in the body, just as devils and angels and heaven and hell exist in the universe. One is the seat of good, while the other is the seat of evil, as the eye is the site of vision, the ear that of hearing, the palate that of tasting, and so forth, as substances and attributes that are located in the human frame.

KM 245

It's a subtle vapor, a fine substance,
A noble and virtuous and good presence.

The *nafs* bears the faculties of life, sense, and volitional motion. The philosopher calls it the animal spirit *(ruḥ-e ḥaiwāni).* It is an intermediary between the heart which is the rational soul *(nafs-e nāṭeqa)* and the body. In the Koran it is referred to as the "blessed tree, an olive neither of the east nor of the west" (XXIV: 35); that is,

1. This term has not been translated due to its wide variety oc connotations. Some of its meanings include: Ego, soul, psyche, spirit, mind, animate being, person, individual desire, personal identiy or self. For a fuller discussion of this concept see the authors *The Psychology of Sufism,* London 1992.

it is neither from the east, meaning the realm of incorporeal spirits, nor from the west, meaning the realm of gross bodies.

It has found a way amongst Turk, Indian and Afghan;
It has found this way through the good auspices of the King.
RSh IV 80

The *nafs* is said to be the essence of the wayfarer, both outwardly and inwardly.

LG

The *nafs* is a subtle, vaporous substance bearing the faculties of life, sense, and volitional motion. It is termed the animal spirit by the philosophers. The *nafs* is, thus, a substance that provides illumination for the body, a light that is cut off, outwardly and inwardly, at the time of death. On the other hand, during sleep the light is cut off only outwardly, continuing inwardly. It has been established that sleep and death are of the same nature, differing in that the latter involves the total severance of the *nafs*, whereas in sleep the severance is only partial.

Consequently, the philosophers distinguish three categories of connection between the substance of the *nafs* and the body. The first is its illumination of all the members of the body, both outer and inner, which takes place in the waking state. Secondly, if the illumination of the *nafs* is cut off outwardly alone, the result is sleep. Finally, if the light of the *nafs* is completely severed, the result is death.

TJ

The grace of God is manifested in the outer form through the sacred spirit, and the wrath of God is manifested through the *nafs*, as in the Koranic passage: "And [God] inspired it [the *nafs]* with conscience of what is wrong for it and what is right for it." (XCI: 8) Those who follow the former course are of the party of the Truth, while those who follow the latter are of the party of what is untruth: "Indeed, is it not God's party who are successful?" (LVIII: 22), and "Indeed, is it not Satan's party who will be the losers?" (LVIII: 19) Of course, God holds the reins of both!

If you want the *nafs* to obey you, then you must obey God, so that He may hand the reins over to you. You must know that the spirit is a light from the realm of God's Grace, possessing both knowledge and power and being characterized by all God's Attributes and characteristics. The *nafs*, however, is not so easily described, for neither can the imagination conceive of it nor is it an objective form which can be grasped.

Indeed, it is an incoming thought *(khāṭer)* from the realm of the Wrath which enters the heart undergoing trial, so that its claim may be realized. It is an imparting *(elqā')* by God, where a flame of the fire of separation is cast into the hearts of the confounded, so that they might know, through the changing of states and the inner journeying, that one must cut away the veils of Wrath, in order to attain witnessing *(moshāhada)* of the manifestations of Grace.

RQR 76

The reality of *nafs* is the inclination of passion towards destructive lust.

SS 614

FREEDOM FROM *NAFS (be-lā nafs)*

He that is free of *nafs* has no trace of blameworthy traits within him and is the possessor of *nafs*-at-rest.

SS 614

THE COMMANDING *NAFS (nafs-e ammāra)*

The term, the commanding soul or *nafs-e ammāra,* has been derived from the Koranic passage: "Indeed, the *nafs* commands one to evil." (XII: 53)

***

The *nafs-e ammāra* is inclined towards corporeal nature, commanding one to the pleasures and passions of the senses and attracting the heart downward. This *nafs* is the abode of evil and the source of blameworthy traits and bad actions. According to the Koran: "Indeed, the *nafs* commands one to evil." (XII: 53)

If the nafs-e ammāra *becomes the commanded,*
Your ruined state will then become cultivated.

RSh IV 80

The *nafs* is called commanding when it heeds the demands of sensual nature with which it comes into contact due to its descent into animal lusts and its ignoring of God's injunctions and prohibitions.

EKJ II 43

The nafs-e ammāra *abases a man,*
If he does not value wisdom.
Sa'di

The *nafs-e ammāra* is that which has not passed the test of asceticism, the skin of its being still un-cured. It is an enemy of the people of God and possesses savage traits. It constantly crawls under the outer cloak of unsuspecting people, and boasts of itself, doing as it wishes. It grazes in the realm of humanity and drinks at the fountain of desire. It does nothing other than eat and drink, fulfilling all the while its own cravings. It appears as a man but is, in reality, a devil. It represents a thick veil between God and His devotees. It destroys religion and is the source of all wrongdoings.

KAM V 92

THE DECEIVING *NAFS (nafs-e makkāra)*

The deceiving soul or *nafs-e makkāra* is weaker than the *nafs-e ammāra* and does not have the power to combat man directly, but is constantly waiting to ambush him. If the disciple is in the station of concentration while traversing the path of striving and asceticism, the *nafs-e makkāra* begins to whisper to him of sacred pilgrimages, presenting them as being more important and advanced than his current station. It may well be right in what it says but it speaks out of deception for its sole desire is to bring the disciple down from his station of concentration and distract him. Sometimes it succeeds and sometimes it does not. If it does succeed, the disciple may never experience concentration again.

This is why followers of the path need a master on the path of devotion, for the master knows the way and its stations, and the traps of the *nafs-e makkāra* are not hidden from him. The master knows the states of his disciples and will guide them accordingly. The elect ones maintain that unless man possesses tranquillity, he is not protected from the *nafs-e makkāra*. Base thoughts arise from the *nafs-e makkāra*.

KAM V 93

THE BLAMING *NAFS (nafs-e lawwāma)*

That nafs *which becomes*
illumined by the heart's light

Turns quickly away
from the darkness of evil action.

The *nafs-e lawwāma* becomes guided by the light of the heart, waking one from the sleep of heedlessness. Through the reforming action of one's state, it wavers between Lordship and phenomenality. So if a bad action is produced by one due to darkness in one's nature, one rectifies it, maintaining blame on the part of the *nafs* through the light of Divine chastisement and awakening, appealing to the All-forgiving, the All-merciful, to be forgiven for base actions. It is in this light that the Koran provides an oath sworn in the name of this *nafs*: "Nay, I swear by the *nafs-e lawwāma...*" (LXXV: 2)

Although this nafs *is moved by one's desire,*
That's not so bad, for it turns to God.

RSh IV 81

The *nafs-e lawwāma* is called the blaming soul at the beginning of its return to God when it refrains from bad things; that is to say, it blames itself for indulging in things where it risks self-destruction.

EKJ II 43

The *nafs-e lawwāma* is the intellect *('aql).*

SS 632

When he has broken the shackles of pride, the *nafs-e lawwāma* is in control.

MM V 2062

THE BEWITCHING *NAFS (nafs-e saḥḥāra)*

The bewitching soul or *nafs-e sahhāreh* lies in wait for the adherents of Reality. When it discovers them engaged in asceticism and worship it declares, "Have mercy on your *nafs,* for it has rights in respect to you."

If the adherent is not a realized one, he will descend from the station of Reality to the station of the religious law and will be granted relief from such hardship. When this relief arrives, however, and the *nafs* is calm and strong, the adherent is returned to the first stage, where the *nafs-e ammāra* is ready to welcome him!

In short, the *nafs-e saḥḥāra* is not that which brings man directly to sin, but rather to worship of the religious law. When he steps on this path of worship, he becomes tainted by his very devotion and the *nafs* whispers to him, "You are better than that evil drunkard!" Upon hearing this, the adherent becomes pleased with himself and looks down upon others, thereby sowing the seeds of his own destruction.

KAM 93

THE *NAFS* -AT-REST *(nafs-e moṭma'enna)*

Rejoice! Good news!
The nafs *has become*
Completely at rest,
a-glow with the heart's light.

At this stage, one has been stripped of the garb of the dissemblence *(talbis)* of blameworthy attributes and dressed in the fine vesture of praiseworthy traits, having become completely focused on the heart. One has advanced in one's progress towards the boundary of the realm of Sanctity, having become free of the evils of dark impurities, assiduous in the observance of devotions, and established in the sublime ranks of God's court, so that one may receive the pleasure of God's address *(kheṭāb).* According to the Koran: "O *nafs-e moṭma'enna,* return to your Lord, content [with God] and contenting [God]; enter among My servants, and enter My paradise! (LXXXIX: 27-30)

Whoever attains such detachment
Is given such honor accordingly.

RSh IV 82

The *nafs* is termed *moṭma'enna* when it has attained tranquillity and repose in God. This occurs when one has completely abandoned unpleasing actions and blameworthy thoughts.

EKJ II 43

The *nafs-e moṭma'enna* is the heart.

SS 632

Become a companion of the nafs-e moṭma'enna,
For the caller-in-the-heart has given it contentment
With the invitation: "Return to your Lord."

Khāqāni

THE FOREMOST *NAFS (nafs-e sābeq)*

The foremost *nafs* is said to be the *nafs-e moṭma'enna.*

ME 6

THE MOST WRETCHED *NAFS (nafs-e ashqā)*

The most wretched *nafs* is said to be the *nafs-e ammāra.*

ME 6

THE OPPRESSING *NAFS (nafs-e ẓālem)*

The oppressing *nafs* is said to be the blaming *nafs-e lawwāma.*

ME 6

THE MODERATE *NAFS (nafs-e moqtaṣed)*

The moderate *nafs* is said to be the inspired soul *nafs-e molhama.*

ME 6

THE INSPIRED *NAFS (nafs-e molhama)*

Know that the inspired soul or *nafs-e molhama* is that which has been graced with Divine inspiration, having also attained the rank of being sworn by an oath in God's Name, as indicated in the Koranic passage: "By the *nafs* and Him Who shaped it, inspiring it with conscience of what is wrong for it and what is right for it." (XCI: 8) The *nafs-e molhama* is that which has occupied the second rank in the realm of the spirits, and is mentioned in the Koran, as well, at the second level: "And among them are those who oppress themselves, and among them the moderate, and among them the foremost in good works." (XXXV: 32)

The name moderate is given to this *nafs*, because it is intermediate between two realms. It belongs fully neither to the realm of the foremost *(sābeq),* who occupy the first rank, nor to that of the oppressive *(ẓālem),* who occupy the third rank. It is the *nafs* of the ordinary friends of God *(wali)* and the elect believers. It has gained the honor of God's inspiration in the realm of spirits in that the spirits of the prophets and elect friends of God have been interposed between it and the Mighty Presence.

When the succor of the Divine emanating grace *(faiḍh-e rabbāni)* came to the spirits of the people of the first rank, a ray from it touched the people of the second rank. Thus, they had some share in the Grace *(loṭf)* and experienced the savour *(dhauq)* of God's address *(kheṭāb)* from behind the veil. When they were joined to this world, even though they were afflicted with the attributes of the *nafs-e ammāra,* still the savour of God's emanating grace *(faiḍh)* had not left the palate of the soul, and the pleasure of hearing God's address *(kheṭāb):* 'Am I not your Lord?" (VII: 172) lingered in the ear of the heart.

ME 359

The *nafs* experiences the utmost level of sensitivity and danger at the station of inspiration. For here it is not completely detached from itself even though it experiences the savouring of the Unseen and Divine inspirations. This may cause pride in the *nafs* assumption that it has reached perfection and may be deceived by the trickery of Satan in looking upon itself as being a worthy and noble being. If this occurs, such a *nafs* becomes the Satan of the age and is blown like a blossom from the tree of acceptance to the earth of baseness by a gale of curses.

ME 363

THE RATIONAL SOUL *(nafs-e nāṭeqa)*

According to the Sufis, the heart may be defined as the rational soul or *nafs-e nāṭeqa.*

SGR 52

The rational soul is an incorporeal substance in one's essence, though associated with corporeality in one's actions, in the manner of celestial souls. When the *nafs* arrives at repose by God's command and its agitation due to the resistance of the passions has disappeared, it is termed at rest *(moṭma'enna).* However, if it has not found repose and still conforms with the sensual soul *(nafs-e shahwāniya),* continuing to object to it, it is termed blaming *(lawwāma),* because its possessor blames himself, for his deficiency in worship of his Lord. Finally, whenever the *nafs* gives up objecting and adheres to the demands of the passions and the claims of Satan, it is termed *nafs-e ammāra.*

TJ

The human rational soul is the site of manifestation of the Divine Names. It is also an intermediate realm *(barzakh)* between the Divine and the phenomenal attributes, as well as encompassing both universal and particular spiritual realities *(ma'nā)*. By means of this comprehensive intermediacy it becomes linked to bodies. It also partakes of both the realms to which it is adjacent, embracing both: that which is purely spiritual and that which is wholly corporeal in terms of space and time. Furthermore, it transcends the change that affects transitory things. Through it, the higher spiritual and the lower corporeal realms are complete. By virtue of its corporeal aspect, it needs time and space and changes with the changing of time and phenomenal things. It is God's vicegerent in the domain of humanity.

RSh IV 308

When the *nafs-e nāṭeqa* witnesses *(moshāhada)* universal and particular spiritual realities, seeing God in them as He should be seen,

It becomes a royal treasure and treasury,
As well as the storehouse of Divine mysteries.

The realized ones know it as the heart, as in the Koranic passage: "Indeed, therein is a reminder for one who has a heart." (L: 37)

The philosophers call it the practical intellect *('aql-e mostafād)*, which is a faculty between the pure intellect and the realm of the ingrained soul *(nafs-e monṭabe'a)*. It takes different forms in each of the five universal Divine realms, representing the Oneness of Concentration *(aḥadiyat-e jam')* in each of the Names, where it appears as a just arbiter.

It is an intermediate realm *(barzakh)* between the outer and the inner, and from it stem both the spiritual and corporeal faculties. It is the Divine form, that is to say, the Unicity *(wāḥediyat)*. Its spirit is the level of the Oneness *(aḥadiyat)*.

RSh II 47

These signs — the earth's swallowing up of sinners, the hurling of stones upon them, and the thunderbolts — were evidence of the might of the rational soul.

MM I 3308

I asked, "Where's the rational soul to be found?"
He replied, "It is found in the subtle world."

Nāṣer Khosrau

THE VEGETATIVE SOUL *(nafs-e nabāṭi)*

The vegetative soul is the first level of perfection of a natural organism, in the sense that it multiplies by reproduction, and requires nourishment. Here perfection, means that which something of a given kind attains within the limits of its own essence. An example of this is the form or quality of a sword as compared to raw iron. The second level has to do with effects or accidents, such as the cutting of a sword, the motion of a body, or the knowledge possessed by a human being.

TJ

THE ANIMAL SOUL *(nafs-e ḥaiwāni)*

The animal soul is at the first level of perfection for a natural organism. It is an agent in the sense that it perceives particulars and moves by its own volition.

TJ

THE HUMAN SOUL *(nafs-e ensāni)*

The human soul is at the first level of perfection for a natural organism. It is an agent in the sense that it perceives universals and performs actions based on thought.

TJ

THE SINGLE SOUL *(nafs-e wāhed yā wāheda)*

The Koran declares, "O Mankind! Be aware of your duty to your Lord who created you from a single soul, and from it created its mate and from them spread a multitude of men and women (IV: 1).

In the realm of ordainment, the single soul represents the first intellect. The Prophet said, "Intellect was the first thing created by God." It itself is a creative object *(maf'ul-e ebdā'i)*, and its mate is the universal soul, which is the manifesting object *(m'aful-e enba'ā'i)*. The result of this union are the detached intellects and souls.

In the angelic realm, the single soul signifies the universal soul and is paired with universal nature. Men are the rational souls while women are the ingrained souls.

In the material realm, the single soul represents Adam and Eve; while men and women are the people of the world, the real human being is the Muhammadan Spirit, who is the Divine representative in the material world.

The Prophet said, "The first thing God created was my light, the light of determined form."

RSh II 55

Dispersion is in the animal spirit; the human spirit is as a single soul.

MM II 188

THE SACRED SOUL *(nafs-e qodosiya)*

The sacred soul is that which possesses the faculty for summoning up the thought of everything that is possible for the human mind to know.

TJ

THE FIRST AND SECOND SOULS *(nafs-e awwal wa nafs-e dowwom)*

The First Soul produced an effect upon the second soul; a fish stinks from the head, not from the tail.

MM II 3080

The second soul is the human soul, the immortal soul of a person, the everlasting spirit of the individual human being.

The First Soul is the First Intellect *('aql-e awwal)* or the Universal Soul *(nafs-e koll),* which is the site of manifestation of determined forms *(ta'ayyon).*

***

THE MONSTER *NAFS (nafs-e ghul)*

The monster *nafs* is the same as the *nafs-e ammāra,* with reference to its ugliness and baseness, as with a demon or devil.

***

On this account [because of the beguiling exposition of a preacher] some Companions begged the Prophet to acquaint them with the deception of the monster *nafs*.

MM I 366

THE ANGELIC SOUL *(nafs-e malakutiya)*

The angelic soul is a spirit characterized by praiseworthy attributes.

D

THE CHASTE AND THE CHASTENED *NAFS* *(nafs-e ẓākiya wa nafs-e ẓakiya)*

The chaste *nafs* is one that has never sinned while the chastened *nafs* is one that has sinned and repented.

KMf 192

THE NUTRITIVE, VEGETATIVE SOUL; THE SENSATE, ANIMAL SOUL; THE RATIONAL, SACRED SOUL; AND THE UNIVERSAL, DIVINE SOUL *(nafs-e nāmiya-ye nabātiya wa nafs-e ḥessiya-ye ḥaiwāniya wa nafs-e nāṭeqa-ye qodosiya wa nafs-e kolliya-ye elāhiya)*

Komail ebn Ziyād recounted, "I asked 'Ali if he could acquaint me with my soul. He countered by asking me which of my souls I wished to know. I exclaimed, 'Are there more than one?! He replied, 'There are four: the nutritive, vegetative soul; the sensate, animal soul; the rational, sacred soul; and the Universal, Divine Soul; and each one has five faculties and two characteristic traits."

1) The five faculties of the nutritive, vegetative soul: retention, attraction, digestion, expulsion, and nurturing. Its two characteristic traits: increase and diminution. The organ in which it is manifested: the liver.

2) The five faculties of the sensate, animal soul: hearing, sight, smell, taste, and touch. Its two characteristic traits: contentment and vexation. The organ in which it is manifested: the heart.

3) The five faculties of the rational, sacred soul: reflection *(fekr),* remembrance *(dhekr),* knowledge, forbearance, and awareness. It has no particular source, although it is the closest thing to the angelic soul *(nafs-e malakiya).* Its two characteristic traits: impeccability and wisdom.

4) The five faculties of the Universal, Divine Soul: subsistence in annihilation, bliss in wretchedness, elevation in abasement, poverty

in wealth, and patience in affliction. It originates from God and to Him it returns. Its two characteristic traits: contentment and submission.

According to the Koran: "And [I] have breathed into him my Spirit," (XV: 29 & XXXVIII: 72) and "O soul-at-rest, return to your Lord, contenting and contented." (LXXXIX: 27 & 28)

KMk 77

THE GROWING, SEEKING AND SPEAKING SOUL *(nafs-e ruyanda wa nafs-e juyanda wa nafs-e guyanda)*

The growing soul is the *nafs-e ammāra.* The seeking soul *nafs-e lawwāma.* The speaking soul the *nafs-e moṭma'enna.*

The growing soul conforms with Wrath in all actions, its actions pleasing Satan. The seeking soul is a heart that is a storehouse of bounty; and the speaking soul is the rational spirit *(ruḥ-e nāṭeqa).*

RQR 76

THE LOVING SOUL *(nafs-e 'āsheqa)*

The loving soul is particular to the prophet, and one of its most perfect attributes is perfection in seeking.

RSh I 348

THE PAUPER SOUL *(nafs-e faqira)*

The pauper soul, which is annihilated from what is other than God, is particular to Moḥammad.

RSh I 349

THE ULTIMATE SOUl *(nafs-e nafs)*

The Ultimate Soul is the inward aspect of Him.

SS 630

NAFS-SLAYING *(nafs-koshtan)*

Nafs-slaying means ridding oneself of the base elements of the *nafs* and Satan by combatting base passions and the desires which stem from them.

***

If you have slain the *nafs*, you are delivered from the necessity of excusing yourself. Nobody in the world remains your enemy.

MM II 785

THE SOUL OF COMMAND *(nafso'l-amr)*

The soul of command signifies the Essential Knowledge that contains all the forms of things, in both their universal and particular aspects, in all their dimensions, both collectively and individually as well as objectively and cognitively.

TJ

THE RIGHTS OF THE *NAFS (ḥoquq-e nafs)*

In Sufi terminology, the rights of the *nafs* are those needs that the *nafs* is dependent upon for its survival.

KF 330

GRATIFICATIONS OF THE *NAFS (ḥoẓuẓ-e nafs)*

From the Sufi point of view, the gratifications of the *nafs* represent those things that are beyond the clear entitlements of an individual.

KF 311

THE PASSIONS *(hawā)*

The passions represent the inclinations of the *nafs* towards the demands of physical nature *(ṭab')* and one's turning away from a loftier perspective and directing one's attention to what is lower.

RSh IV 27[1]

The passions represent the inclination of the *nafs* towards that which it finds sensuously pleasing without attention to the principles of the religious law.

TJ

The passions represent the inclination and desire of the *nafs* for those things that are agreeable to it and that it covets in such a way as to cause one to forget one's seeking [on the Path].

---

1. ES 46.

The house of the nafs
is a paradise full of passions;
The house of the heart
is the dwelling-place of veracity.

TT

The reality of the passions is the lust of the *nafs*, which is its inclination for that which gives it comfort and keeps it away from that which gives it discomfort.

The term passions generally indicates opposition to God. It may also be employed in the pure sense of inclination *(mail),* involving loving-kindness towards God, as well as what is other than God, or in the sense of God's particular loving-kindness and one's compliance therewith. This last connotation is the one current among the Sufis.

The *Ṣaḥā'ef (Journals),* states that passion represents one of the levels of loving-kindness, where the heart is in constant desire for the Beloved, and is a station of five degrees: 1) meekness *(khoḍhu'),* 2) pledging one's life blood in worshipping the Beloved to an intensity beyond endurance, as did the Prophet when, in the course of daily prayers *(namāz),* he would stand so long that both his feet swelled up, sometimes standing on tiptoe and sometimes suspending himself in position, and giving himself over to remembrance *(dhekr);* 3) patience in time of adversity and trial, as the expression goes: "Patience gulps down the affliction of which one does not complain"; 4) supplication; and 5) contentment and submission.

KF 1543

According to the opinion of some, the passions constitute a term applied to the attributes of the *nafs*, but according to others, they represent a term denoting the natural volition whereby the *nafs* is controlled and directed, just as the spirit is controlled by the intellect. Every spirit that is devoid of the power of the intellect is imperfect and causes distance from God while every *nafs* that is devoid of the power of the passions is closer to God and less powerful.

Man is continually being called by the intellect and the passions to contrary ways. If he obeys the call of the intellect, he acquires faith and Divine Unity, but if he obeys the call of the passions, he falls into error and disbelief. Therefore, the passions are a veil for those who would reach God, a site of deviation for disciples, and a domain where seekers turn away from God, and the devotee is commanded to resist them. As the saying goes: "Whoever follows the passions is destroyed, while whoever opposes them dominates."

According to the Koran: "But as for one who feared to stand before his Lord and restrain his *nafs* from the passions..." (LXXIX: 40). The Prophet stated, "Indeed, what is most to be feared is that which I fear from my community: namely, the following of the passions and persistence in expectations."[1] It is related that, in commenting on the passage: "Have you not seen one who has made his passions his god, and God leads him astray?" (XLV: 23) Ebn 'Abbās said, "That is to say that the passions are a god that one worships." Woe be to one who worships his passions rather than God, where all his aspiration *(hemmat)* is devoted day and night to seeking to satisfy them!

KM 260

The passions of the *nafs* are a cincture *(zonnār),* impeding the progress of the *nafs* towards perfection. Such a *nafs* impedes the advancement of the heart, as well. In being held back by the passions, the *nafs* prevents the heart from moving forward into traversal of higher stations.

TKQ 388

When, from fear of God, you have relinquished the passions, the goblet to drink from God's heaven will arrive.

MM VI 3501

Ignorance in childhood
may not be not counted;
Drunkenness in youth
may be indulging the passions.

'Attār

Every step taken
to trample the worldly nafs
Means two steps taken
in the spiritual domain.

Maghrebi

1. SEM Ḥodud 13.

The most manifest attribute of the *nafs* is lust, which is dispersed in different parts of the human body, and is served by the senses. The devotee must guard all his members from it, and he shall be questioned concerning the acts of each. The lust of the eye is sight, that of the ear is hearing, that of the nose is smell, that of the body is touch, and that of the mind is thought. It behooves the seeker of God to spend his whole life, day and night, in ridding himself of these incitements to the passions *(hawā),* which show themselves through the senses, and to pray to God to make him such that this desire will be removed from his inward nature, since whoever is affected with lust is veiled from all spiritual things. If the devotee should try to repel it by his own exertions, his task would be long, for it is persistent in all its forms. For the goal to be attained, the way is submission .

KM 263

Lust is the activity of the *nafs* in seeking what agrees with it.

TJ

The intellect is contrary to lust. O brave man, do not call intellect that which involves lust.

MM IV 3301

Show me a man who is restrained at the time of anger and lust; I have been searching for such a one from one street to the next.

MM V 2893

According to a Sacred Tradition, where the Prophet recounts God's words to him: "Whenever My devotee becomes primarily engaged with Me, I turn his lust into entreaty of Me and communion *(monājāt)* with Me." The lover's lust is no more than love, loving-kindness, and gazing at God's Beauty. Lust is a special thing in the lover, existing solely in the vision *(ro'yat)* of the Beauty, for viewing the Splendor and the Grandeur burns up the lust of the lover.

Jonaid said, "The vision of Splendor and Grandeur causes intimacy to vanish from the hearts of His friends."

The gnostic said, "Human lust is the steed of spiritual lust which, in turn, is the steed of the lust of love; and the lust of lovers is the longing of spirits for the realm of spiritual joys."

MA 136

THE HEART-ORIENTED SOUL *(ru')*

The term *ru'* is sometimes used by the Sufis to refer to that aspect of the soul that is focused on the heart, which some identify with the breast *(ṣadr)*.

NK 35

PHYSICAL NATURE *(ṭab')*

Physical nature is the constitutional foundation on which each human being has been created.

TJ

What is physical nature?
Falling from clay to clay,
Sticking like a donkey to the single track.

MN 44

If you want the Beloved to remain your Beloved,
Seek His temperament and manner of conduct.

HH 448

THE HEART *(qalb yā del)*

The heart is an incorporeal luminous substance, intermediate between the spirit and the *nafs*. It is through this substance that humanity becomes realized. The rational soul *(nafs-e nāteqa)* is the philosophers term for this luminous substance, which we call the heart.

The animal soul *(nafs-e ḥaiwāni)* is the philosopher's term for the steed on which the heart is mounted, and is understood to stand between the rational soul and the body, as in the relationship between the glass and the shining star, where the spirit is the lamp, in the passage: "The example of His light is as a niche wherein is a lamp; the lamp is in a glass; the glass is, as it were, a shining star, [the lamp] lit from a blessed olive tree, neither of the East nor of the West...." (XXIV: 35).

The tree is the perfected soul and the niche the body. In between the two, in terms of being and in terms of the hierarchy of revealed things, the heart serves as the Guarded Tablet in the world.

Learn epitomized knowledge from the heart
And differentiated knowledge
from the tablet of the soul.

RSh IV 144-145

The heart is one of the names of the spirit, constituting a rank in the hierarchy of the spirit, according to the gnostics. At this rank the heart moves between two aspects, focusing one way on God seeking emanating grace *(faiḍh)* from the lights thereof, and the other way on the animal soul *(nafs-e ḥaiwāni),* upon which it bestows the grace it has received. The names and ranks that the spirit enjoys in the human world include the following: the inner consciousness *(serr),* the arcane *(akhfā),* the spirit itself, the heart, the word *(kalema),* the heart-directed soul *(ru'),* the site of heart-vision *(fo'ad),* the breast *(ṣadr),* the *nafs*, and the intellect. In the macrocosm it enjoys such names and levels as the First Intellect, the Sublime Pen *(qalam-e a'lā),* the Light, the Universal Soul, the Guarded Tablet, and so forth.

NK 24

The heart is said to represent the attribute of total comprehensiveness, of the all-embracing, of all-inclusiveness which is a manifestation of the comprehensiveness of the external Existential Attributes. Because of this it is capable of serving as a vehicle for the display of theophanies of the Beauty and the Majesty: "My earth and sky cannot encompass Me; yet the heart of My devotee contains Me." [1]

How silent it has become in the house of the heart!
The heart as hearth and home
has encompassed the world.

It is a tavern of ruin beyond the two worlds;
The winehouse of the heart
is there forever.

TT 196

The heart is a Divine subtlety that is connected to the cone-shaped physical heart, which is located on the left side of the breast. This subtlety is the reality of man. In philosophical terms it is the rational soul. The spirit is the inner aspect of the heart, and the animal

---

1. *Traditions of the Prophet,* Vol. I, p. 25.

soul its steed. Man's faculty for perceiving and knowing is the heart, which also serves to receive God's address *(kheṭāb),* His calling to account and reproach.

TJ

Know that the heart connotes the heart of the gnostic-in-God, for the gnostics do not consider the physical heart to be the heart in the truest sense, merely a figurative version thereof.

NN 198

The heart is a site of Divine seeing —
Within which are illumined decorations and carpets.
What you figuratively refer to as 'heart':
Go throw it before the dogs in the street!
The heart which is greater than the intellect
Is not that which has the shape of a cone.

HH 340

The heart is the quintessence of the human soul. It is a mirror, enclosed by the two worlds. By its reflection, all the Attributes of Beauty and Majesty of the Divinity are manifested.

When the human soul, in its capacity as a mirror, has been nurtured and brought to perfection, it witnesses *(moshāhada)* the manifestation of all the Attributes of God within itself.

ME 3

All subtle material nourishment was taken and made into the human body; and all subtle material in the body was taken and made into the form of the heart. All subtle material in the human spirit was taken and made into the soul of the heart.

The heart, thus, became the quintessence of the two worlds, corporeal and spiritual, and hence, too, the locus of the manifestation of gnosis. Thus, according to the Koran: "He inscribed faith in their hearts." (LVIII: 22) No other part of man was fit to receive the Divine inscription nor worthy of being 'held between God's two fingers'.

ME 146

The heart is the site of manifestation of the Name, the Just. It is concerned with regulating the body, the *nafs*, and all the corporeal and spiritual faculties. Nothing in the hierarchy of Being is as fundamental to matters, both outer and inner, as the heart, which is the form of the Oneness of Concentration *(aḥadiyat-e jam')* between the outer and the inner. Hence, it has become the site of manifestation of all the Divine levels. It is through the heart that man becomes all-embracing and acquires perfections.

Know that in reality the heart is the World-viewing Cup;
Both the greater and the lesser are manifested within it.

The heart is the mirror of the essence of the Majestic;
In the heart of the pure one God displays His Beauty.

Heaven and earth cannot encompass God;
But He can be contained in the believer's heart.

No one has seen the limits of the heart's domain;
It serves as a sign of God's Comprehensiveness

The heart is the Divine station
Manifesting God's station as it actually is.

Because the heart, by virtue of its serving as a median between the outer and the inner, brings together all opposites, the poet says:

The two worlds are combined within it;
Sometimes Satan, sometimes Adam.

Since the human heart is the site of manifestation of the Divine Concentration, the truths of the levels, outer and inner, that constitute the two worlds have been brought together in the human heart. All the pairs of Divine Names, Majestic and Beautiful, have become manifested therein according to the hearts capacity. The Names manifest at every instant according to the varying dictates governing them, each time displaying a different nature. At times, in being dominated by the Majestic Names, they become Satan, who is the site of manifestation particular to those Names, and at other times, under the influence of the dictates of the Beautiful Names, they become Adam, in whom the Beautiful Attributes are dominant and the Majestic ones suppressed. Due to its embracing of such extremes, the heart is never long in one state, every moment in a different world, every instant displaying a different Attribute and nature.

In every corner there are a hundred idol-temples,
On every side a hundred Ka'bas and sites of worship.

Sometimes it circulates
around the upper realm;
Sometimes it's situated
in the lower realm.

Sometimes detached from nature,
sometimes involved with it,
Sometimes it's linked with God,
and sometimes separated.

Sometimes it becomes an angel,
sometimes a baleful devil;
Sometimes it is pure intellect,
sometimes it is the nafs.

SGR 119

Dā'ud Qaiṣari, a commentator on Ebn 'Arabi, states: "The heart refers to one of the levels of the rational soul *(nafs-e nāteqa),* within which it may witness *(moshāhada)* spiritual realities *(ma'nā),* whether universal or particular, whenever it wishes. It is this level which the philosophers call the practical intellect *('aql-e mostafād).*"

Given this, one must be aware that the term heart in the usage of the gnostics in general, and in the usage of Ebn 'Arabi in particular, is employed with a broader connotation than that indicated above. Heart represents the all-encompassing human reality, embracing all levels of existence. Further gnostic connotations of the heart are: the site of manifestation of the Identity *(howiyat)* of the Essence, Names and Attributes, and the site of manifestation of the Divine Justice; the form of the Oneness of Concentration *(aḥadiyat-e jam')* between the outer and the inner, where the heart is more extensive than the earth, the sky, and even the Divine Mercy which, in the final analysis, is the Throne of the Compassionate. Herein, oncethe heart becomes purified, polished, and purged of all impurity, all knowledge, particularly that which is involved in gnosis and knowledge of God, becomes revealed.

EA 176

In Sufi terminology, when the human heart witnesses spiritual realities, universal and particular, it is said to be the rational soul. The philosophers call this level the practical intellect. They ascribe a heart to one who is characterized by praiseworthy traits.

The heart of the gnostic has always been referred to as the Greatest Name *(esm-e a'ẓam),* in terms of its turning back and forth among the realm of pure intellect and that of engendered souls *(nofus-e monṭabe')* and the five universal Divine realms. The heart involves the Oneness of Concentration, being a medium between the outer and the inner. The spiritual and corporeal faculties emanate from it.

The heart is the form of the level of the Oneness *(aḥadiyat)*. Through its perfection and comprehensiveness all things, including both God and the creation, are contained, although it is not contained within itself.

RSh IV 301

The heart is a Divine spiritual subtlety that is linked to the physical heart, in the way that accidents are linked to substances or attributes to the things that they qualify. It is the reality of a person. Wherever the heart is mentioned in the Koran or the Prophetic Custom *(sonnat)*, it is with this connotation. Elsewhere the word heart may be used with the connotation of *nafs* or spirit or intellect, but the fundamental sense is the above-mentioned. Other meanings are figurative. Jāmi states in his commentary on the *Foṣuṣ al-ḥekam*: "The heart is a reality that relates corporeal realities to the bodily faculties and spiritual realities to characteristics of the *nafs*."

KF 1170

THE LOVER'S HEART *(del-e 'āsheq)*

The lover has a heart that transcends determined form *(ta'ayyon)* and that is enshrouded by the Might. It is the confluence of the seas of the realm of the Unseen and the visible realm.

This heart has such an aspiration that
If it drinks a thousand cups of wine as vast as the sea,

Still its aspiration would continue
to seek to drink more wine.

In fact its expanse is such that not only can the whole universe not contain it, but the whole universe vanishes into insignificance in its grasp! God erects the pavilion of the Singularity *(fardāniyat)* on the courtyard of the Uniqueness *(wāḥediyat)* of the heart, establishing the court of the Monarch there and accomplishing His works there. The loosening and the binding, the contracting and the expanding, the fluctuation and the stabilizing, all are brought to light there.

When He contracts,
He hides what He has revealed;

When He expands,
He restores what He has hidden.

***

I'm amazed at how the Beloved,
Whom, due to His beauty, the world can't contain,
Keeps setting up a household
in the cramped confines of my heart.

Bāyazid indicated the vast expanse of his heart when he said, "If the Throne and all it contains were placed in a corner of the gnostic's heart, the gnostic would be unaware of it."

Jonaid said, "If the transitory were to be joined to the Eternal, not a trace of it would remain. When Bāyazid looks into such a heart, in which there is no trace of the transitory, he sees only the Eternal. That is why he exclaims, "Glory be to Me!"

Lm 36

SPIRITUAL LEVELS OF THE HEART *(aṭwār-e del)*

The heart has seven spiritual levels *(ṭaur).*

The first spiritual level of the heart is called the breast *(ṣadr),* which is the repository of the jewel of Islam, where the Koranic passage speaks of "one whose breast God has opened up for surrender (Islam) to Him, so that he followeth a light from his Lord." (XXXIX: 22) When it is deprived of the light of Islam, the breast becomes a repository of darkness and disbelief, as with "one who opens the breast to disbelief." (XVI: 106) It becomes the site of the temptations of Satan and the enticement of the *nafs*, that "whispers in the breasts of people." (CXIV: 5) Of the aspects of the heart, it is only the breast that being, as it were, the skin of the heart, can become the site of temptations and enticement, for these have no access to the interior of the heart, which is God's treasury and resembles the heavens, to which such things have no access: "We have guarded them from every accursed devil." (XV: 17)

The second spiritual level of the heart *(del)* is called the heart *(qalb)* properly speaking, and is the repository of faith *(imān),* where "He inscribed faith in their hearts." (LVIII: 22) The heart is the site of the light of the intellect, with reference to those who "have hearts with which to feel." (XXII: 46) It is also the site of insight, where it "is not the eyes that grow blind, but the hearts, which are within the breasts, that grow blind." (XXII: 46)

The third spiritual level is the pericardium *(shaghāf),* which is the repository of loving-kindness, love and compassion towards ones fellow creatures: "He enamored *(shaghafa)* her with love." (XII: 30) Loving-kindness towards one's fellow creature does not pass beyond the pericardium.

The fourth spiritual level is said to be the heart-site-of-vision *(fo'ād),* which is the repository of witnessing *(moshāhada)* and the site of vision *(ro'yat):* "The *fo'ād* did not lie about what it saw." (LIII: 11)

The fifth spiritual level is known as the grain of the heart *(ḥabbato'l-qalb),* which is the repository of loving-kindness for the Divinity *(oluhiyat).* It belongs to the elect, who have no room in them for the love of any created being.

The sixth spiritual level is known as the core of the heart *(sowaidā'),* which is the repository of Divinely inspired knowledge *('elm-e ladoni).* It is the source of wisdom, the treasure house of Divine mysteries, and the site of knowledge of the Names: "And He taught Adam all the Names." (II: 31) In it are unveiled the varieties of knowledge to which the angels are not privy.

The seventh spiritual level is called the heart-blood *(mohjato'l-qalb),* which is the repository for the manifestation of the lights of theophanies of the Divine Attributes. This is the mystery of "We have honored the children of Adam," (XVII: 70) a form of honoring *(karāmat)* that was conferred on no other species of beings.

ME 195

PROSTRATION OF THE HEART *(sojud-e qalb)*

The prostration of the heart is the annihilation of the devotee in God in the course of contemplative vision of God in such a way that the action of the limbs does not distract him or cause his vision to cease.

RSh IV 87

POSSESSOR OF HEART *(ṣāḥeb-e qalb)*

The term, the possessor of heart, refers to one in whose heart knowledge has accumulated so that no tongue, however eloquent, can express it.

It is reported that Jonaid said, "The people of Khorāsān are possessors of heart."

LT 359

EXPANSE OF HEART *(sa'ato'l-qalb)*

Expanse of heart represents the realization by the perfect man of the reality of his intermediate position, embracing both the levels of contingent being and Necessary Being. For the perfect man the heart is this very intermediate realm *(barzakh)* referred to in the Sacred Tradition: "My earth and heavens cannot encompass Me; yet the heart of My believing devotee contains Me."[1]

RSh IV 91[2]

THE HEART OF BEING *(qalbo'l-wojud)*

According to Ebn 'Arabi, the heart of being is the perfect man.

MjS 921

THE SEVEN SPIRITUAL STAGES *(aṭwār-e sab'a)*

According to the Sufis, the seven spiritual stages are those of physical nature *(ṭab')*, the *nafs*, the heart, the spirit, the inner consciousness *(serr)*, the arcane *(khafi)*, and the most arcane *(akhfā)*.

KF 907

THE SPIRIT *(ruḥ)*

In Sufi terminology, the spirit has two connotations:

1) One of the seven spiritual stages *(aṭwār-e sab'a)*, standing between that of the heart and that of the inner consciousness *(serr)* and constituting a stage of progress, of ascent, of the psyche *(rawān)*.

2) The human heart in the absolute sense, which is called *jān* (soul) in Persian.

***

In the terminology of the Sufis, the spirit is a subtlety that is human and incorporeal. In the terminology of physicians, it is a vapor

1. *Traditions of the Prophet*, Vol. I, p. 25.
2. ES 103.

that is subtle, born of the heart, and capable of being endowed with the faculties of life, feeling and motion. This is also referred to as the *nafs*. The Sufis believe that between the spirit and the *nafs* stands the heart, which perceives both universals [as does the spirit] and particulars [as does the *nafs*].

The coin of the heart is called counterfeit
in the sense that it turns from this to that;
Sometimes it is found in the precincts of the Ka'ba;
sometimes it is drunk in the temple of the Magi.

The philosophers do not distinguish between the heart and the first spirit, and call both the rational soul *(nafs-e nāteqa).*

RSh IV 151

The realized ones have a different view of the spirit than that of the exoteric ones. Some maintain that it is no more than life itself. Others hold that spirits are subtle essences that have been consigned to the forms they have. According to Divine tradition, as long as the spirits are in bodies, these bodily forms possess life. A human being is alive because they posses a spirit, while a spirit is consigned temporarily to a body. Spirits are able to develop during sleep, when they take leave of the body, then return. The human being consists of both spirit and body, and both will be accountable on the Day of Judgement. At the meeting place of the two, the human being partakes of each in turn. The spirit is a created being. To call it eternal is a grievous error. Some maintain that the spirit is the repository of good, while the *nafs* is the repository of evil, and that the intellect constitutes the army of the spirit and the passions the army of the *nafs*. God-given success provides succor for the spirit, while despair feeds the *nafs*. Finally, the heart serves as a supportive army that conquers all else.

JAZ 148

THE SUPREME SPIRIT *(ruḥ-e a'ẓam)*

Know that the noblest being, the object of vision closest to the Divine Might, is the Supreme Spirit, which God ascribes to Himself with references, "of My Spirit: (XV: 29) and "of Our Spirit." (LXVI: 12)

The Adam, the First Vicegerent, the Divine Interpreter, the Key to Existence, the Pen of Creation, and the Paradise of Spirits are all attributes of the Supreme Spirit, its essence being the first to fall prey into the net of being.

The Divine Will has appointed the Supreme Spirit to be its vicegerent in the realm of creation, entrusting it with the keys to the treasuries of the mysteries of being, and placing them at its disposal. The Supreme Spirit opened a mighty river to itself from the sea of life, so that it is forever afforded support by the emanating grace *(faiḍh)* of life, pouring grace, in turn, upon the particles of phenomenal existence.

Furthermore, the Supreme Spirit conveys the forms of Divine words from the locus of Concentration *(jam‘)*, that is, the Sacred Essence, to the site of dispersion, which is the realm of creation, and radiates from the essence of summation into the essences of differentiation.

The Divine Honoring *(karāmat)* has conferred two eyes *(naẓar)* upon the Supreme Spirit: one for the witnessing *(moshāhada)* of the Majesty of the pre-eternal Power, and the other for contemplating the Beauty of the everlasting Wisdom. The first *naẓar* represents the innate intellect *(‘aql-e feṭri)*, which is mentioned in the Prophetic Tradition that states that God told the Supreme Spirit to advance, while the second *naẓar* represents the created intellect *(‘aql-e khalqi)*, which is a guide. According to the tradition, "Turn towards me and it did and returned." From the former springs Divine loving-kindness, while from the latter derives the Universal Soul *(nafs-e kolliya)*. The Universal Soul receives every grace for which the relative spirit *(ruḥ-e eḍhāfi)* appeals from the essence of Concentration, become the site of differentiation. Due to the interaction between the relative spirit and the Universal Spirit, the relationship of male and female comes into being, reflecting the dual tendencies of activity and passivity, of strength and weakness, and the process of mutual attraction and coming together is established. Through their commingling in mating the phenomena of existence are born, brought into the visible realm out of the placenta of the Unseen by the hand of the midwife of ordainment. Hence, all created entities are the products of the Universal Soul and the Spirit [in its relative form]. The Universal Soul itself derives from the Supreme Spirit, which, in turn, is produced by the Command *(amr)*, for God has created the Spirit directly without any secondary cause, this being the implication of the Command, while all other created entities have been brought about by means of the Spirit, as in the Koranic reference:

"Indeed, His is all creation and the Commandment!" (VII: 54)

Since it is evident that each vicegerent is a combination of all the diverse characteristics, God in His universal Grace *(faḍhl)* and infinite Munificence has clothed the Spirit, enjoying the vicegerency of creation, with the vesture of all His Names and Attributes, both Beautiful and Majestic, honoring and dignifying it with the throne of His creation.

When the circle of creation reached its final point, corresponding to the initial point, the form of the Spirit was reflected in the mirror of the being of earthly Adam, and all the Divine Names and Attributes became manifested in him.

Then God's declaration, "Indeed, I am about to place a vicegerent on earth" (II: 30) was heard, and the announcement of Adam's vicegerancy was broadcast from the lofty places. Inscribed on the writ of proclamation of his vicegerancy were the words: "Indeed, God has created Adam in His image" and on the standard of God's honoring *(karāmat)* appeared this passage: "And He taught Adam all the Names." (II: 31)

MH 94

The level of the spirit is the shadow of essential unity, and the level of the heart is the shadow of Divine Unity, while the Supreme Spirit, that is, the human spirit, has various manifestations and names and belongs to both macro and micro realms. The first effect that originates from the Real is the Supreme Spirit which is the link between being and non-being, as indicated by the words of the Prophet, "God has created no creation more supreme than the spirit."

The Supreme Spirit is a Divine luminous essence. With respect to its essential quality, it represents the single soul, as indicated in the Koran, "Your Lord who has created you from a single soul." (IV: I) With respect to its luminosity, it represents the First Intellect, as indicated by the words of the Prophet, "The first thing God created was the Intellect."

The first person in whose form the Supreme Spirit manifested was Adam, and the first person in whose form the universal soul manifested was Eve. In the same way that the Supreme Spirit is referred to as the First Intellect with respect to its luminosity, the universal soul is referred to as the Second Intellect because of its darkness.

The Supreme Spirit has a number of names and manifestations.

It is called the Pen for it manifests words from the Divine Essence of Concentration to the differential plane which is the Universal Soul. It is also called the Breath of the Merciful, for the Merciful has bestowed spirits upon all bodies of the world through the supreme spirit at the command of, "I blew my spirit into them...". (XV: 29) The soul is the substance behind the forms of words. The spirit is the substance behind the forms of words bestowed by God upon the human spirits as indicated in the Koran, "I inculcated the word to Maryam and her spirit." (IV: 171)

RSh I 285

The Supreme Spirit is the human spirit as the site of manifestation of the Divine Essence in its aspect of the Lordship *(robubiyat)*. It is impossible for the human spirit to hover around the Essence or to desire union with it. Only God knows the core of His Essence. This is a mystery known only to God. The Supreme Spirit is the same as the First Intellect, as well as the Moḥammadan reality, the single soul *(nafs-e wāḥediya)*, and the reality of the Names. It is the first being which God created in His own image. It is also the greatest vicegerent *(khalifa-ye akbar)*. A luminous essence, its essential nature serves as the site of the manifestation of God's Essence and its luminosity serves as the site of the manifestation of God's Knowledge. Moreover, in terms of its essential nature, it is known as the single soul, and in terms of its luminosity, the First Intellect.

Just as the Supreme Spirit enjoys manifestations and names in the macrocosm, such as the First Intellect, the Sublime Pen, the Guarded Tablet, and so forth, likewise, in the microcosm, on the human plane, it enjoys manifestations and names in terms of its outward nature and levels such as: inner consciousness *(serr)*, the arcane *(khafā')*, the spirit, the heart, the Word, the heart-oriented soul *(ru')*, the heart-site-of-vision *(fo'ād)*, the breast, the intellect, and the *nafs*.

TJ

God's Supreme, Antecedent, First and Last Spirit is known as the First Intellect.

ES 152

THE HUMAN SPIRIT *(ruḥ-e ensāni)*

The human spirit is a knowing and perceptive subtlety possessed by human beings and dominating the animal spirit *(ruḥ-e ḥaiwāni).* It has descended from the realm of the Command *('ālam-e amr).* The intellect is incapable of perceiving its core. Being incorporeal, this spirit is engendered *(montabe')* in the human body.

TJ

THE SPIRIT OF IMPARTING *(ruḥo'l-elqā')*

The spirit of imparting being Gabriel, is that which imparts *(elqa')* knowledge of things in the Unseen to the heart. It may also represent the Koran, in so far as referring to the Koranic passage: "The Lord of the Throne imparts the spirit of His Command to whomever of His slaves He wills." (XL: 15)

RSh IV 151

THE RATIONAL SPIRIT *(ruḥ-e nāteqa)*

The rational spirit is the soul *(nafs)* that witnesses inspiration.

SS 632

THE SPIRIT OF SPIRITS *(ruḥo'l-arwāḥ)*

According to Ebn Arabi, the Spirit of Spirits has the general meaning of the Perfect Man *(ensān-e kāmel)* and the specific one of the Moḥammadan reality *(ḥaqiqat-e moḥammadiya).*

MjS 542

THE WORLD-SPIRIT *(ruḥo'l-'ālam)*

The World-Spirit is synonymous with the World-Heart *(qalbo'l-'ālam)* and the Heart of Being *(qalbo'l-wojud).*

***

According to Ebn 'Arabi, the World-Spirit signifies the Perfect Man *(ensān-e kāmel),* or in another context, Moḥammad alone.

MjS 543

THE UNIVERSAL SPIRIT *(ruḥ-e koll)*

According to Ebn 'Arabi, the Universal Spirit is the same as the Breath of the Merciful *(nafas-e raḥmāni).*

MjS 545

THE SPIRIT OF ME *(ruḥo'l-yā')*

According to Ebn 'Arabi, the Spirit of Me is that refered to by the Koranic passage: "And I breathed into him of My Spirit," (XXXVI-II: 72). The *yā'* (y) My is the letter appended to *ruḥ* Spirit, to read *ruḥi* (My Spirit) hence signifying God's identification of the Spirit with Himself.

MjS 546

THE SPIRIT OF GOD *(ruḥo'llāh)*

The Spirit of God is said to represent Jesus, on the basis of the Koranic passage: "Then We sent unto her Our Spirit, and it assumed for her the likeness of a perfect man. (XIX: 17)

***

You are the Kheḍhr of the time and the Succor *(ghauth)* of every ship in distress; do not, like the Spirit of God [Jesus], practice solitude.

MM IV 1461

There was a Christian girl,
of spiritual nature, who enjoyed

A hundred recognitions
in the way of the Spirit of God.

MT

THE HOLY SPIRIT *(ruho'l-qodos)*

The Holy Spirit represents Gabriel, as in the Koranic passage, "Say: the Holy Spirit has revealed it from your Lord with Truth, that it may confirm those who believe, and act as a guidance and good tidings for those who have surrendered." (XVI: 102)

***

There is more to say, but the Holy Spirit will speak to you of it, not me.

MM III 1298

When all became
Illumined by God's light,

The Holy spirit then cried out,
"O Woe! If I go further my Lord,
This flame will burn my feathers still more!"

AN 20

THE TRUSTED SPIRIT *(ruḥo'l-amin)*

The Trusted Spirit normally refers to Gabriel, although occasionally in Rumi's Mathnawi it may represent the Moḥammadan spirit:

"Since the name of Aḥmad [Moḥammad] became [to the Christians] an impregnable fortress, what then must be the Essence of that Trusted Spirit?"

MM I 738

It may also signify the Master of the Path or the Perfect Man:

If that Trusted Spirit spills my blood, I'll drink drought upon drought of blood, like the earth.

MM III 3891

THE SPIRIT OF THE LANDS *(ruḥo'l-belād)*

In his Mathnawi, Rumi uses the term, the Spirit of the Lands, to refer to the person of Moḥammad:

"When I beheld you, O Spirit of the Lands, love for this earthly sun fell from my eye."

MM VI 1085

THE ANIMAL SPIRIT *(ruḥ-e ḥaiwāni)*

The animal spirit is a subtlety, the source of which is the cavity of the corporeal heart. It is diffused through the veins to the other parts of the body.

KF 548

Dispersion is at the level
of the animal spirit,
While the single soul
is at the level of the human spirit

MM II.)

THE REAL SPIRIT *(ruḥ-e 'ain)*

The real spirit signifies the human spirit *(ruḥ-e ensāni)* in its highest form, namely, as the true and essential soul *(jān-e ḥaqiqi wa dhāti):*

Between every two way-stations *(manzel)* yonder, there is a distance a hundred times that from the vegetative state to the real spirit.

MM V 806

THE ETERNAL SPIRIT *(ruḥ-e qadim*

The Eternal spirit represents the ultimate spirit, the Koran, and the light of witnessing. According to the Koran, "And thus we have inspired in you [Mohammad] the spirit of our command."(XLII: 52)

SS 630

THE SPIRIT OF REVELATION *(ruḥ-e waḥy)*

The spirit of revelation involves the Divine revelation *(waḥy-ye elāhi),* which is particular to prophets and friends of God *(wali):*

The spirit of revelation is more concealed than the intellect. Because it is of the Unseen; it belongs to that side.

MM II 3258

THE *NAFS'* SPIRIT AND SENSATE SPIRIT *(ruḥ-e nafsāni wa ḥassās)*

The rational soul *(nafs-e naṭeqa)* has an organ located beside the base of the brain, known as the *nafs* or, sensate spirit. It was created for the purpose of serving as an organ for the rational soul. It is the organ of imagination *(khayāl),* estimation *(wahm)* and reflection *(fekr).*

RSh I 298

THE INNER CONSCIOUSNESS OR MYSTERY *(serr)*

It is probable that the inner consciousness is a subtle entity within the framework of the body, similar to the spirit, serving as the site of witnessing *(moshāhada),* just as the spirit is the site of loving-kindness and the heart that of gnosis, these functions having been predicated by the purposes for which they were created.

It has been said that a person has no control over the inner consciousness, while only God knows the workings of the ultimate inner consciousness *(serr-e serr).* One group maintains that, on the basis of the purpose for which the two faculties were created, the inner consciousness is subtler than the spirit which, in turn, is nobler than the heart.

RQ 134

The inner consciousness is a subtlety that has been consigned to the heart, as the spirit has been to the body. It is the site of witnessing, just as the spirit is the site of loving-kindness and the heart that of gnosis.

TJ

Inner consciousness means concealment of feelings of love.

KM 500

The inner consciousness is an arcanum between non-existence and existence. No tongue can describe the reality of it. The gnostic knows it directly, without intermediary, but cannot disclose what he knows. These are the secrets revealed in the unveiling *(kashf)* of the realm of sovereignty *(molk)* and the angelic realm *(malakut).*

SS

The inner consciousness is higher than the spirit, being the sacred angelic intellect *('aql-e qodosi-ye malakuti).* Its site is the subtlety of God which has been consigned to the spirit. It is by means of the inner consciousness that the spirit comprehends the unveiling *(kashf)* of the Attributes that flow to the inner consciousness from the realm of God. It is the site of the spiritual realities of Divine Knowedge.Thwhich is revealed to it is hidden from the spirit and the heart. That which enters it is called mystery, for it is a secret of God's knowledge that touches inner consciousness without involvement of the spirit.

According to the Koran: "And God knows what you proclaim and what you hide." (V: 99 & XXIV: 29) The Prophet stated, "God has a mystery in the hearts of His friends of which no intimate angel is aware." Concerning the fundamentals of the Sufis, the master has said, "The inner consciousness is subtler than the spirit, which, in turn, is nobler than the heart."

The gnostic said, "The inner consciousness is the site of the lights of witnessing *(moshāhada).*"

MA 153

The inner consciousness is an arcanum between non-existence and existence, on the plane of spiritual realities *(ma'nā).* The ultimate inner consciousness *(serr-e serr)* is that which the inner consciousness *(serr)* cannot sense. Sahl ebn 'Abdo'llāh said, "The *nafs* has a mystery that God has made known only through the tongue of Pharaoh, when he proclaimed, "I am your Lord, the Highest." (LXXIX: 24)

LT 354

The inner consciousness is that which the consciousness of the *nafs* cannot sense. God has kept it concealed, keeping watch over it Himself. Some maintain that the inner consciousness is of two kinds: God's, which He watches over directly, and that of creation, which He watches over through intermediaries. It has also been held that the inner consciousness applies to the ultimate inner consciousness *(serr-e serr),* which is God, Who appears only to Himself; and that what appears to the creation is not the inner consciousness.

LT 231

The inner consciousness of the lover contemplates *(morāqaba)* God's mysteries, which He has called the Unseen, which is hidden to the inward eye, being revealed only to the eye of the inner consciousness. This concerns elect unveiling *(kashf)* and elect knowledge.

The gnostic said, "Vision *(ro'yat)* of the inner consciousness involves visionary revelation of special Attributes in the guise of lights."

MA 126

Whenever one enjoys contemplative vision *(shohud)* of God so one's consciousness becomes purified and made free from existential things, one becomes the repository of the mysteries of the Names, Attributes, and Essence, by having attained stability *(tamkin)* in gnosis and constancy in servanthood *('obudiyat)* and the perception of Lordship *(robubiyat).* God speaks to the gnostic through the pre-eternal knowledge and eternal information that he had deep within him, revealing to him thereby the mystery of what has been ordained in the Unseen. Then the eye of his inner consciousness becomes bright with the collyrium of the light of God's mystery. He contemplates God through God's mystery and God's mystery through God; and he speaks of God's mystery to God. Through his inner consciousness he attains the ultimate inner consciousness, about which God informed His cherished one [Moḥammad], when He confided in him with the outward tongue of His inner consciousness and inward aspect, saying, "Although you may speak aloud, indeed, He knows the inner consciousness and the more arcane *(akhfā),*" (XX: 7) where the more arcane is the ultimate inner consciousness.

Then the Prophet described the Chieftains *(noqabā')* among the people of Reality and the Substitutes[1] *(bodalā')* of gnosis, saying, "They are the repositories of the mysteries." Certain masters have said that the inner consciousness senses that which the *nafs* cannot.

It is related that Yusof ebn Ḥosain said, "The hearts of men are the graves of mysteries," and "If my breastbone learned of my inner consciousness, I would rip it out and cast it away." It has been said that inner consciousness arises from the ultimate inner consciousness, which is God, who appears only to God, while whatever appears to the creation is not inner consciousness.

It is recounted that Ḥosain ebn Manṣur [Ḥallāj] said, "My inner consciousness is inviolate, and the fantasy of the one who fantasizes cannot penetrate it."

The gnostic said, "God has in His Acts mysteries which have been discovered by the philosophers. These mysteries are the subtleties of the pre-eternal Wisdom in the arrangement of the forms of existence. Furthermore, God has in His Attributes mysteries which have been discovered by the gnostic thinkers. These spiritual realities *(ma'nā)* are the Names under which are classified knowledge of Divine ordainment. Finally, God has in His Essence mysteries which have been discovered by the elect adherents of Divine Unity. These are the lights of the truths that God has revealed to the people of God."

MA 158

It has been said that the creation is based on veiling *(ḥejāb).* If the veil were to be lifted, creation would be obliterated. On the other hand, the inner consciousness is based on witnessing *(moshāhada).* When it becomes veiled, it is obliterated. The inner consciousness is

---

1. One of the levels of sainthood, within the hierarchy of saints described by various Sufi Masters, such as Sanā'i, Ruzbehān, Jāmi, and Ebn 'Arabi. It usually denotes a saint who after their death would be substituted for by another person. Some masters say they nunber seven and others say there are forty.

the opposite of what is outward."

KST 160

The inner consciousness is the level and limit that God gave each thing when He was creating it. God's words in the following Koranic passage refer to this: "Indeed, Our word to a thing, when We intend it, is only that We say to it, Be!, and it is." (XVI: 40)

It has been said that only God knows God, loves God, and seeks God, where the inner consciousness is the vehicle for seeking, loving, and knowing God, hence the Prophet's statement: "I have known my Lord through my Lord."

ES 100

The inner consciousness is said to be something connected to the Unseen, being hidden from the intellect.

When one is in touch
with the inner consciousness,
One can travel straight from
particular to Universal.

TT 206

In the early stages, the inner consciousness involves knowing what is hidden by means of avoiding hypocrisy and becoming purified. In the final stages, it involves annihilation in the pre-eternal Identity *(howiyat).*

RSh IV 180

One school of Sufis hold that the inner consciousness is one of the subtleties of the site of witnessing *(moshāhada),* just as the spirit is a subtlety at the site of loving-kindness and the heart at the site of gnosis. Another school maintains that the inner consciousness is not an essence *('ain)* but a spiritual reality *(ma'nā),* that is to say, a hidden state between the devotee and God, of which no one else can be aware.

It is said that the devotee enjoys an inner consciousness of God, while the innermost consciousness is the more arcane, as in the Koranic passage: "And if one speaks aloud, indeed, He knows the inner consciousness and the more arcane." (XX: 7) The inner consciousness is that of which no one but God and the devotee are aware; and of the innermost consciousness not even the devotee is aware, unless he is a one who knows the realm of the inner consciousness and arcane things *('ālemo's-serr wa'l-khafiyāt).*

Concerning the above mentioned first schools who consider the inner consciousness to be a particular essence, some hold that it is higher than the spirit and the heart. Others maintain that it is higher than the heart, but lower than the spirit. Sohrawardi's belief is that the inner consciousness is not a separate entity from the heart or the spirit. It has been said that the reason the one school holds that the inner consciousness is higher than the spirit is that they consider the spirit, after complete liberation from bondage to heart and base attachments, to be an attribute that becomes added to something higher. What they do not understand is that it is the spirit itself that is characterized by something foreign to it. As for those who contend that the inner consciousness is lower than the spirit and higher than the heart, their error is that they consider the heart, in having become completely liberated from the humility of enslavement to the *nafs* and delivered from the clinging of base worldly motivations *(hājes)* and Satanic temptations *(waswasa),* to be an attribute of a foreign entity which they conceive to higher than the heart.

Others have given the inner consciousness another interpretation, namely, that it is a subtle spiritual reality *(ma'nā)* hidden in the core of the spirit, impossible for the intellect to interpret, or at the core *(sowaidā')* of the heart, inaccessible to description by the tongue, where, as the tongue is the interpreter and expresser of the heart, so the intellect is the interpreter of and commentator upon the spirit.

MH 101

The Eighty-third Field is the Inner Consciousness, which proceeds from that of Detachment from Self *(enferād).*

According to the Koran: "And God knows their inner consciousness." (XLVII: 26)

The inner consciousness is that epitome of humanity that one possesses with God, and the hidden thing that the tongue can never express and which is that part of oneself about which one cannot give account. It is of three kinds:

1) That which is hidden to others, being service in retreat, of which there are three conditions: knowledge of the science of service, not violating the rights of others, and keeping ones presence from offending others. For whoever does not observe these, retreat is transgression.

2) That which is hidden to the angels, being visionary disclosure *(mokāshafa)* of Reality, of which there are three signs: expanse of

the heart to receive the Power, seeing the darkness of others' excuses, and opening one's eyes to God's bounties.

3) That which is hidden to oneself, which is annihilation in Union *(mowāṣela)* with God. This is a flashing glance, whereby the devotee comes to focus the eye of his heart on God with one of three motivations: fear of something, hope of something, or love of something, this something being God, where everything other than Him is nothing, non-existent.

SM

According to the Koran: "God knows best what is in their hearts." (XI: 31) Those who possess inner consciousness are those described in the Prophetic traditions as being hidden.[1] They are of three ranks or degrees:

1) Those whose aspiration *(hemmat)* is lofty, whose aims are pure, and whose conduct is correct. They are not recognizable by any outer convention, are not ascribed any particular name, nor can they be pointed out. They are God's treasures, wherever they may be found.

2) Those who give indication of being at one station but are really at another, who show themselves to be involved in one matter when they are really engaged in another, and who announce themselves to be undertaking one task when they are really concerned with another. They possess a jealousy that veils them, an etiquette that protects them, and a subtlety through which they will have been refined.

3) Those whom God keeps hidden from themselves, bathing them in such an aura that they cannot perceive where they are, making them so confounded in infatuation that they cannot see what they are about, and so conceals their state from their intellect that they cannot know what is happening to them. Although they possess testimonies *(shawāhed)* whereby they can see their station truly, these are kept in their inner consciousness. Such testimonies include sincere intention, which tends towards the Unseen; sincere love, the knowledge of which is hidden from them; and an other-worldly ecstasy, the fiery source of which remains hidden to them, and this is the rarest station of the friends of God.

MS

---

1. *Aḥadith-e Mathnawi,* Fruzanfar, no. 91.

In the early stages the adherents of the inner consciousness traverse the inner consciousness in the Eternal pre-eternal realm, after experiencing witnessing. The adherent is plunged into the sea of the core of the Essence and Attributes and witnesses the Might within Might and Grandeur within Grandeur in one instant.

The gnostic said, "The traversal of the inner consciousness never ceases in eternity and occurs at every moment."

MA 260

THE DETACHED INNER CONSCIOUSNESS
(serr-e mojarrad)

The detached inner consciousness is that which is purified of awareness of the inner consciousness *(serr).*

SS 568

The detached inner consciousness is that in which awareness of the transitory does not occur. It is founded in God and beholds nothing other than Him, as where the Prophet is described in the Koranic passage: "And the eye did not swerve, nor was it overbold." (LIII: 17)

The gnostic said, "The station of the detached inner consciousness is that of God and of nothing else. It is filled with God, leaving no room for anything other than Him."

MA 281

THE MYSTERY IN THE INNER CONSCIOUSNESS
(serr dar serr)

The external aspect of the mystery in the inner consciousness is inspiration *(elhām)* in expansion, and its reality is in the bestowal of awe.

SS 568

THE MYSTERY OF KNOWLEDGE, OF STATE, AND OF REALITY
(serr-e 'elm, serr-e ḥāl, serr-e ḥaqiqat)

Harken to discourse
on the mystery of those who know;
I counsel your heart
to listen through the soul.

According to the people of God, mystery is of three levels: that of knowledge, that of state and that of Reality.

The mystery of knowledge through God involves the epitomizing of opposites as one essence. The word, *'ālem* (one who knows), is linked with the word, *'alāmat* (sign) where God is the One who Knows of the world *('ālam)* through the knowledge *('elm)*, which is enjoyed by the one who knows His Essence, and every individual who knows is a sign of one of the Divine Names.

All things point to His Names;
Each shows a particular Name.

The mystery of each thing is the summation and subtle form of that thing, the hidden reality therein. The principal essences *(a'yān-e thābeṭa)*, which are the forms of the Divine Names, exist on the plane of the knowledge of the mysteries of Lordship *(robubiyat)*, which itself is the relationship between the Lord, or one who nurtures *(rabb)*, and the nurtured *(marbub)*.

Once the worshipping devotee completes the required observances to the fullest, he engages in supererogatory good works, ultimately entering the circle of God's intimates, being included among the lovers of God.

God bestows eyes and ears upon him,
And grants him perfect knowledge as well.

At this point, the mystery of state is revealed, where the Guide and the guided become one.

Finally, the mystery of Reality is where one becomes aware that the knowledge of God is not additional to God's Essence, for the possessor of the mystery of Reality becomes the one who Knows of the world *('ālem-e 'ālam)*. The eye of Reality sees through God, whereas the mystery of knowledge [namely, the Knowledge] is an Attribute of God and state is one of the things that can be known of the Knowledge. The Knowledge is all-encompassing and state is which is encompassed. Being robed in the guise of Lordship, the mystery of state must declare:

I am the one who loves Me,
and the one who loves Me is I;

We constitute two spirits,
integrated in one body.

The one who knows distinguishes between knowledge, the itself, and the world, where the mystery of knowledge is more complete than the mystery of state, and the mystery of Reality is more complete that the mystery of Knowledge.

If you count yourself
among the dervishes,
Then you must understand
well their mystery.

If you understand the mystery
of knowledge and state,
You truly
comprehend perfection.

RSh IV 199

THE ULTIMATE INNER CONSCIOUSNESS *(serr-e serr)*

The ultimate inner consciousness is that which distinguishes God from the devotee. An example of such is knowledge of both the differentiation and summation of truths within the comprehension of Oneness, and knowledge relating to God only known to Himself, as indicated in the Koranic passage: "And with Him are the keys to the Unseen; no one but He knows them." (VI: 59)

TJ

The ultimate inner consciousness is that which is sensed by the gnostic's spirit and from which it takes pleasure, causing exhilaration *(enbesāṭ)*, which it cannot show to the intellect.

SS 574

The ultimate inner consciousness is the internal aspect *(bāṭen)* of the reality of gnosis.

SS 631

VISION OF THE ULTIMATE INNER CONSCIOUSNESS *(ro'yat-e serr-e serr)*

The inner consciousness *(serr)* has an eye, which is directed towards the ultimate inner consciousness *(serr-e serr)*. Its vision *(ro'yat)* consists in the appearance of the Attributes to the inner consciousness *(serr)* in the course of unveiling *(kashf)* of the Essence. This revelation occurs when love departs from the lover.

The gnostic said, "The vision of the ultimate inner consciousness is the description of what clearly appears in revelation."

MA 127

GNOSIS OF THE ULTIMATE INNER CONSCIOUSNESS *(ma'refat-e serr-e serr)*

What we have cited of the inner consciousness represents the site of ultimate inner consciousness *(serr-e serr),* which is the site of elect theophany. The knowledge of the inner consciousness belongs to the Names and Attributes of God. According to the Koran: "He knows the inner consciousness and the more arcane." (XX: 7)

The masters have said that the inner consciousness is that which one may perceive, while the ultimate inner consciousness is that which other than God cannot know.

The gnostic said, "The ultimate inner consciousness is one of the degrees of the Ultimate Unseen."

MA 154

THE ARCANE OR TRANS-CONSCIOUSNESS *(khafi)*

In Sufi terminology, the arcane or trans-consciousness is a Divine subtlety that has been consigned in potential to the spirit. It can be acquired in its realized form only after one has been overwhelmed by Divine infusions *(wāred).* Once such overwhelming has taken place, the intermediary between God and the spirit, after accepting theophany of Divine Attributes and emanation of God's special grace *(faiḍh),* turns towards the spirit.

TJ

THE MOST ARCANE OR SUPER-CONSCIOUSNESS *(akhfā)*

The most arcane or super-consciousness is called such because its reality is hidden *(ekhtefā)* from the gnostic and anything else. Ruzbehān says that the most arcane is the same as the ultimate inner consciousness *(serr-e serr).* It appears that this term has been derived from the Koranic passage: "And when one speaks aloud, indeed, He knows the inner consciousness *(serr)* and the more arcane *(akhfā).*"(XX:7)

The most arcane is the final stage in the progress or advance of a person's psyche.

***

Now, the hidden spirit *(ruḥ-e khafi)* is called the arcane by the wayfarers. It is a light more subtle than the inner consciousness *(serr)* or the spirit, being closer to the realm of Reality. This is not the conventional spirit, for this is more subtle than all other spirits; rather, it is a spirit that applies specifically to the elect.

KF 542

Where does the *nafs* fit into the arrangement of the treasury of the heart? What does the heart know of the subtleties in the sanctum of the spirit? What does the spirit know of those things that have been entrusted to the pavilion of the inner consciousness? What does the inner consciousness know of the truths contained in the arcane? Now, the *nafs* is the site of the trust *(amānat),* the heart the home of gnosis, the spirit the sign of witnessing *(moshāhada),* and the inner consciousness the site of the abiding of love. Only God knows what the most arcane is and who is aware of it. It is beyond ordinary people's powers of conception and comprehension.

KAM VI 112

Knowledge Gnosis Wisdom and Perfection

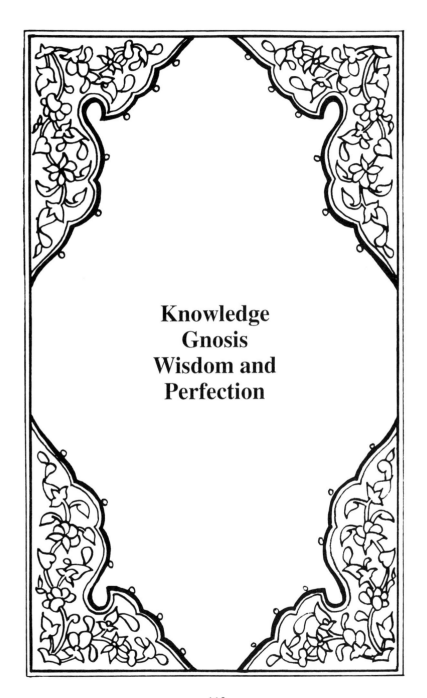

KNOWLEDGE (*'elm*)

The Sufis are not concerned with exoteric fields of knowledge and outer conventions, which are based on imitation and repetition. They consider only authentic those fields of knowledge that involve knowledge acquired through purification of the *nafs*, refinement of temperament, and expansion of the heart.

They believe that exoteric knowledge engenders doubt and uncertainty constituting, in fact, the greatest veil. The sole knowledge that is useful and beneficial is that which brings one close to God. Hence, the knowledge the Sufis are concerned with is that of love and spiritual state, not verbal disputation.

***

The knowledge of the heart elevates one; the knowledge of the body weighs one down. When knowledge strikes on the heart, it becomes a helper; when knowledge strikes on the body, it becomes a burden.

The knowledge that is not directly from Him does not last, it is cosmetic.

MM I 3446-3447 & 3449

In fact, the Sufis prefer not to use the word, knowledge, where it implies awareness on the part of the brain. According to Hojwiri,[1]

1. KM 68.

masters of the Path call knowledge that which is "stripped of spiritual meaning and devoid of spiritual practice."

It has also been said that true knowledge does not spring from the pen, but comes from what God pours into the heart.

RAj 29

Once I had become manly
in seeking the Beloved,
The first step was to become alien to all being.
God would not listen to knowledge, so I shut my mouth;
God would not accept intellect; as a result, I became crazy.

Abu Sa'id Abe'l-Khayr

Knowledge involves the exact correspondence of firm belief with actuality. The sages have said the following about knowledge: it is the acquisition of the form of a thing in the intellect; it is the perception of something as it really is; it is the emergence of the known from the hidden, where ignorance is the opposite; it requires no definition; it is the fundamental attribute by which universals and particulars are perceived; it signifies the *nafs*' attainment of the spiritual reality *(ma'nā)* of something; it signifies the coming of the intellect and its Object into conjunction; and that it signifies an attribute that possesses attribution.

TJ

Knowledge is an essential perception of one's own reality, life, and being. It represents one's perception of the realities of known things in their essential form through total comprehension.

Nafato'r-ruḥ wa toḥfato'l fotuḥ 50

Knowledge, property, office, rank and fortune bring trouble in the hands of the evil-natured.

MM IV 1438

What is knowledge? Making an atom important,
And spinning round and round till post-eternity.

MN 45

In the early stages, knowledge means the Shari'at which is acquired through practice and persistence. In the final stages, it means the contemplative vision *(shohud)* of God from His Essence to His Essence. This is known as the vision of certitude *('aino'l-yaqin)* and the perfection of the station of beneficence *(eḥsān).*

RSh IV 177

Abu 'Ali Thaqafi said: "Knowledge is the heart's coming alive out of the death of ignorance; it is the light that brightens the eye of certitude out of the darkness of infidelity."

KM 19

Sufi masters have said that the reality of knowledge is that which is revealed to the inner consciousness.

TA 802

The ultimate stage of knowledge is ignorance; that of reason, bewilderment; and that of gnosis, submission.

TKQ 348

Knowledge is the instrument for ensnaring the devotee, for it is the means by which a person is drawn into the snare of Divine servanthood.

TKQ 299

DEGREES OF KNOWLEDGE *(darejāt-e 'elm)*

The first degree of knowledge is that of reality which is followed by that of the essence of reality, and then the truth of reality. The knowledge of reality is gnosis of God, that of essence of reality is Being, and that of the truth of reality is annihilation. Gnosis is comprehension, Being is attainment, and there are a thousand waystations between the two.

KAM VII 196

THE CONVENTIONS OF KNOWLEDGE *(rosum wa roqumo'l-'olum)*

The conventions of knowledge are one's cognitive faculties. The conventions are the Divine Names, such as the All-knowing, the All-hearing and the All-seeing, which are external, mounted on the bodily frame. The cognitive faculties may be likened to vessels, arrayed in the hereafter, between God and the creation. Thus, given that these are God's Effects and Attributes and the conventions and forms of His Names, whoever comes to know oneself and one's attributes fully comes to know God, according to the Tradition: "One who knows himself knows his Lord."

RSh IV 150

THE PEARLS OF PERCEPTION, OF KNOWLEDGE, AND OF UNION *(zawāhero'l-anbiā' wa zawāhero'l-'olum wa zawāhero'l-weṣla)*

The pearls of perception and knowledge represent the gnosis of the Path, which is the noblest and most luminous of the fields of knowledge. The pearl of Union is attained through God and requires knowledge of the Path.

RSh IV 37

THE OUTER ASPECT OF KNOWLEDGE *(ẓāher-e 'elm)*

From the point of view of the realized one, the outward aspect of knowledge is the essences of contingent beings.

KF 930

THE MYSTERY OF KNOWLEDGE *(serr-e 'elm)*

The mystery aspect of knowledge is the reality therein. Knowledge in its true sense is God Himself, being other than Him only from the point of view of what is transitory.

ES 101

GOD'S KNOWLEDGE *('elm-e ḥaqq)*

Being signifies the Great Book, while Knowledge is the Universal Incorporeal Reality. It possesses relations, particulars, laws, accidents, and preconditions. The All-knowing is one of the Essential Names. The Knowledge is distinguished from the Absolute Unseen in being the level of the determined form *(ta'ayyon)* of the Name.

The Knowledge is that which reveals things, while the Unseen of the Essence enjoys name, attribute and level only in terms of external manifestations and levels. The Knowledge is also the essence of light, through which God may be seen and what is other than God known. Because of the intensity of its appearance, the Knowledge is unknowable, for the precondition of knowing is that the one who knows be greater than, as well as antecedent to, the Known, and therefore antecedent to the Knowledge of the Unseen of the Essence. Hence, the Knowledge is known through the Unseen of the Essence. The antecedence of the relation of the Life to the Knowledge is conditional upon their differences. The antecedence of the relation of the Life to the Knowledge is itself based on Knowledge, according to the Tradition: "Only God knows God."

The one who knows the Essence is
Is Essence Itself;
How could Knowledge and the Known
be other than the Essence?

RSh I 267

DIVINE KNOWLEDGE (*'elm-e elāhi*)

Divine knowledge is that which engenders the knowing of the states of beings that have no inherent need of matter. In other words, it is a knowledge which in itself has no need of matter.

TJ

KNOWLEDGE OF SUFISM (*'elm-e taṣawwof*)

Knowledge of Sufism
is never exhausted;
It is sublime,
celestial, Divine.
It contains benefits
for those who know it,
those of pure style,
of special craftsmanship.

Knowledge of Sufism is never exhausted, that is, in terms of its benefits, not quantitatively. It is inspired, not acquired. Since it is provided by One Who is infinite, its support is limitless. It is the resplendence of nobility, glory, and elevation. This knowledge is sublime in the sense that it refers back to God; and it is noble insofar as it is known.

It is said to be celestial and Divine because it is immediate, being directly inspired in the devotee by God. Communication through angelic intermediaries is the revelation from God to the prophets. Communication on the part of the prophets is their mission *(resālat),* where they serve as intermediaries between God and people. Once again, the inspiration that God infuses in the heart of the devotee is without intermediary.

This knowledge contains benefit for those who possess it, that is, if a Sufi, one may benefit from this knowledge.

The knowledge of Sufism is known by one who is complete, chosen, and elect.

KST 257

OBTAINED KNOWLEDGE *('elm-e ektesābi)*

Obtained knowledge is that which is acquired by means of secondary causes.

TJ

CONJECTURAL KNOWLEDGE *('elm-e ẓanun)*

Conjectural knowledge is that which is based on conjecture, such as external knowledge, obtained knowledge based on philosophical speculation, and the like, which are mixed with uncertainty.

FLM

Amongst the sources of the Masters there is no dispute, such as there is in conjectural knowledge.

MM VI 4135

THE TRANSCRIBED KNOWLEDGE *('elm-e katib)*

The transcribed Knowledge is that of the Text, the Book, the external manifestation of the Koran.

FLM

How long will you steal portions of the transcribed Knowledge, in order that your face may be colored like an apple?

MM VI 128

TRANSMITTED KNOWLEDGE *('elm-e naql)*

Transmitted knowledge is that which is related by one person to another, being equivalent to knowledge which has been handed down *('elm-e manqul)*, such outer knowledge, and exoteric knowledge, as the sciences of jurisprudence, the principles of religion, commandments of the Shari'at, and the like.

FLM

Had he had been filled less with transmitted knowledge, and had carried away from a Friend the knowledge of revelation to the heart, he would have gained deliverance.

MM IV 1416

ACTIVE AND PASSIVE KNOWLEDGE
('elm-e fe'li wa 'elm-e enfe'āli)

Active knowledge is that which has not been acquired from someone else, as opposed to passive knowledge, which has been acquired from someone else.

TJ

Active knowledge is that which prompts the actualization of what is known, such as when one is standing on a wall and fear of falling causes one to actually fall, or when the conception of things desired brings about the desire for them.

Passive knowledge is that which involves the knowing of something already in existence, such as that which is the subject of our sciences about externally existing objects.

SMH 159

IMPRINTED KNOWLEDGE *('elm-e enṭebā'i)*

Imprinted knowledge involves the knowing of something after the appearance of its form in the mind. In this sense, it may be referred to as acquired knowledge *('elm-e ḥoṣuli).*

TJ

PRESENTIAL KNOWLEDGE *('elm-e ḥoḍhuri)*

Presential knowledge involves the knowledge of something without appearance of its form in the mind, such as a person's knowledge of himself.

TJ

THEOLOGY *('elm-e kalām)*

Theology is the science of the fundamental principles of Islam.

TJ

UNVEILING KNOWLEDGE *('elm-e kashfi)*

Those who attain knowledge say that it is more complete than spiritual state. The Sufis hold that spiritual state is more complete. This is the author's [Shāh Ne'mato'llāh] view. Unveiling knowledge is more complete than spiritual state. State is more complete than acquired knowledge and may be subject to pretense while knowledge is not. The Prophet was commissioned to seek increase in knowledge, as in the passage: "Say: My Lord, increase me in knowledge!" (XX: 114) Divine theophanies are infinite, and each one requires the knowledge of something, and each piece of knowledge requires a savouring *(dhauq)*.

RSh II 158

Unveiling knowledge is to acquired knowledge as the wellspring is to a mirage. As the Prophet stated: "Those who attain knowledge are the heirs of the prophets."[1]

There is the inherited knowledge,
and there is acquired knowledge;
Your knowledge is transmitted;
mine is the savour of Divine friendship.

The doctors of conventional knowledge and the elders with practical wisdom are ennobled by what has been transmitted *(manqul)* to them and invested with the subtle raiment of what they have reasoned *(ma'qul),* but they are denied the crown of God's honoring *(karāmat)* and the cincture of gnosis of the infinite Names and Attributes, and are not clothed with the Divine temperament. The most knowing one, the Prophet, stated: "I have been taught the knowledge of the first things and the last."

RSh II 165

THE KNOWLEDGE OF VISIONARY DISCLOSURE *('elm-e mokāshafa)*

The knowledge of visionary disclosure is knowledge of the inner and the ultimate knowledge. It is the knowledge of the sincere and those intimate with God. It is the light that appears in the heart in the

1. *Traditions of the Prophet, op. cit.*, vol. I, p. 50.

course of its ablution and purification from blameworthy attributes. When the light appears, a multitude of things are revealed, accompanied by True gnosis of the Essence of God and of its Eternal and Perfect Attributes. Furthermore, one comes to understand God's disposition of things with respect to created existence in both worlds, the knowledge of the spiritual realities *(ma'nā)* of prophetic mission and the Prophet, and the manifestation of angels to the prophets. One also knows the nature of the arrival of prophetic revelation to the angels and the angelic realm *(malakut)* of the heavens and the earth, this last being the disposition of people who come to enjoy different stations with respect to the spiritual realities of these things, once they have confirmed acceptance of the principles governing them.

The aim of the knowledge of visionary disclosure is to lift the veil, so that God's presence becomes directly observable *('eyān)* to the possessors of this knowledge, such that doubt and uncertainty are utterly banished from them. The acquisition of this kind of knowledge by human beings is made possible only if the mirror of the heart is not stained with the impurities of the world, and is free of corrosion.

EA 177

UNIVERSAL KNOWLEDGE *('elm-e kolli)*

Universal knowledge is said to be the Divine Knowledge.

KF 1264

KNOWLEDGE THROUGH ALLUSION *('elm-e eshārat)*

Knowledge through incoming thoughts *(khāṭer),* witnessing *(moshāhada)* and visionary disclosure *(mokāshafa)* all come under the category of knowledge through allusion.

Whatever this term covers is not qualified, limited or describable. Thus, the spiritual reality *(ma'nā)* of what appears in the gnostic's inner consciousness *(serr)* has been put there by God. It is not God Himself. Whatever can be described cannot represent precisely what God expresses as spiritual reality in allusion. Furthermore, where God cannot be expressed verbally, neither can He be alluded to by any allusion. God's allusions can be known only by the gnostic whose inner Divine characteristics, externally, reveal his station.

If God projects for the gnostic the witnessing of the inner in a state of fear, his outer state will reflect this; likewise with the state of hope, and so forth.

Since knowing for the gnostic is solely through allusion, the spiritual reality that appears to him is known as knowledge through allusion. One must be aware that expression is the effect of allusion, that outer movements are the effect of inncoming thoughts. By the same token, knowledge through allusion comes in terms of incoming thoughts which, like transitory beings, last no more than a moment *(waqt)*.

If witnessing *(moshāhada)* were to last more than a moment for the inner consciousness *(serr)*, the gnostic would be so overcome [by that state] that the Shari'at would be neglected. Thus, witnessing involves a display and a withdrawal. When display takes place, the gnostic experiences it. When it disappears, the charismatic effects remain.The witnessing that the inner consciousness enjoys today becomes visionary disclosure *(mokāshafa)* of the Essence tomorrow.

When vision becomes direct observation *('eyān)*, it becomes annihilated from all the spiritual realities of the devotee. The Shari'at is shed. Then God appears tranquilly to the inner consciousness, so that it may not be without the Beloved. God snatches away what remains of the Shari'at [in the devotee], for it is the outer adornment of servanthood, and when one's servanthood is not so adorned, one's inner being is not in order. Since this knowledge involves a display and a snatching away, it is termed knowledge through allusion.

This knowledge through allusion is one that is exclusive to the Sufis; that is, only they possess it, no one else. This comes about after the other kinds of knowledge which we have cited have been experienced by them. The reason why they have termed it knowledge through allusion is that witnessing by the heart and visionary disclosure to the inner consciousness cannot be described as they really are. This is to say that when something is witnessed by the heart and visionary disclosures to the inner consciousness are fully realized, no further expression is possible.

KST 255

THE KNOWLEDGE OF CONDUCT ON THE PATH *('elm-e soluk)*

The knowledge of conduct on the Path involves the *nafs'* awareness of matters of conscience which favor or oppose it in the light of what it has known previously. It is also called ethics *('elm-e akhlāq)* or knowledge of Sufism *('elm-e taṣawwof).*

The *Majma'as-Soluk (Compendium of the Path),* states: "The noblest of the fields of knowledge is that of truths, waystations, and spiritual states. It is the knowledge of spiritual practice and ethics in the course of the performance of devotions and of attention to God from every point of view. This knowledge is called the knowledge of conduct on the Path."

KF 32

KNOWLEDGE OF COMPREHENSION
('elm-e fahm)

Knowledge of comprehension is different from exegesis and hermeneutics *('elm-e tafsir wa ta'wil),* for it comes through instruction and inculcation. Hermeneutics *(ta'wil)* involves Divine guidance and God-granted success. Comprehension comes directly through Divine inspiration. With exegesis no instructor is involved. Hermeneutics requires spiritual endeavour. One who comprehends has only one teacher: God. Exegesis and hermeneutics require science and striving, whereas comprehension simply befalls one and attracts.

When one of the Companions asked the Prophet the meaning of inner knowledge *('elm-e bāṭen),* that is, knowledge of comprehension, he explained that it "is a form of knowledge between God and His friends *(wali)* and is not shared by even the intimate angels or any of God's devotees." Furthermore, the comprehension of the Book and the Custom *(sonnat)* on the part of those men of God is such that the illusion *(wahm)* of the exotericist dares not venture into the vicinity of its sacred confines! For them, every letter of God's Word contains a station, every word provides a message, every verse brings new mastery, and every chapter gives both pain and joy. On their Path, God's threat is a blessing, and His blessing is their realization.

KAM VI 292

KNOWLEDGE OF SPIRITUAL STATE
('elm-e ḥāl)

Of the various kinds of knowledge particular to the Sufis, one is knowledge of spiritual state. This is the perpetuation of contemplation by the heart and the inner consciousness *(serr)* and the form of the given state between the devotee and God. Knowledge of spiritual state involves consideration of the qualitative and quantitative aspects thereof in all spiritual moments based on a counterbalanced increase, decrease and uniformity of spiritual state, as well as the strengths and weaknesses thereof. This, in turn, is measured by the criterion of sincerity, so that at every moment the requirements thereof may be observed and the corrEsponding etiquette maintained, for every spiritual state has its own etiquette, varying with each moment and being consistent with the etiquette of the relevant spiritual station.

MH 69

KNOWLEDGE OF CAPACITY *('elm-e sa'at)*

Whenever the temperament of the *nafs* is transformed and the demon of one's physical nature submits to Islam, where compliance with the passions is replaced by obedience to God, some of one's pleasures turn to rights. At this point, the way is opened to depart from the straits of constraint *(ḍharurat)* into the expanse of capacity. The Sufis call this level the station of amplitude.

This state is realized either at the beginning of the station of the annihilation of self-will, the station of abandonment of volition, or at the station of subsistence through God, after the annihilation of one's individual being.

MH 73

KNOWLEDGE OF CONSTRAINT *('elm-e ḍharurat)*

In Sufi terminology, knowledge of constraint signifies perception of what is necessary for the *nafs* in motion and at rest, as well as what is necessary in the course of speech, action, and awareness during the period of imprisonment for the *nafs* at this station. The limit of what is necessary for the *nafs* should not be denied, because it is its right. To deny the *nafs* its rights is unacceptable. A right of the *nafs* is something that if denied will not create a breach of religious or of worldly requirements. A reference to this right was made by the Prophet, when he stated, "Indeed, your *nafs* has a right which you must respect."

MH 71

CONVENTIONAL KNOWLEDGE *('elm-e rasmi)*

Conventional knowledge is said to be that which relates to rational and worldly matters.

***

Abandon conventional knowledge,
for it's all talk, all chatter;
Give me the lesson of love, O heart,
for it's all ecstasy and state!

Shaikh Bahā'i

Finally Bahā'i
got down to business;
In the assembly
of love he scorned reason.
He tore up the books
of conventional knowledge
And threw all the pages
out of the window.

Shaikh Bahā'i

KNOWLEDGE OF ETIQUETTE *('elm-e ekhlāq)*

In the terminology of the knowledge of conduct on the Path *('elm-e soluk)*, knowledge of etiquette is a practical wisdom that refines the temperament. It is also known as material wisdom *(ḥekmat-e khalqiya)*.

KF

KNOWLEDGE OF GOD'S SUPPORT *('elm-e qiām)*

From the point of view of the Sufis, the knowledge of God's support is where the devotee, in all his periods of motion and rest, both outer and inner, sees God as supporting, as being aware of him, considering that God is watching over him in all his states, speech, and action. This term is derived from the Koranic passage: "Is He Who supports every *nafs* in what it acquires...?" (XIII: 33)

The sign of this knowledge is that the devotee keeps his outer and inner being constantly graced with the adornment of the etiquette of conformity with Divine commandments, being divested of the garb of opposition. This is also referred to as the knowledge of watchfulness *(elm-e morāqabat).*

Sahl ebn 'Abdo'llāh Tostari said, "Be not wanting in these four things: 1) the knowledge of God's support, such that you see God watching over, and aware of you in every state; 2) perseverance in servanthood, such that you are constantly dedicated to an attitude of servanthood; 3) continuous seeking of God's help in granting you success in observing the first two above; and 4) persistence in patient observance of all these until death."

MH 68

THE KNOWLEDGE OF MOMENTS *('elm-e auqāt)*

Jonaid said, "The noblest of activities is to teach spiritual moments. This involves the knowledge that protects one's *nafs*, heart and religion."

TA 440

FIGURATIVE AND TRUE KNOWLEDGE *('elm-e majāzi wa 'elm-e ḥaqiqi)*

Shaikh Bahā'i uses the terms, figurative and true knowledge for conventional love and knowledge of love respectively:

You who are accustomed
to figurative knowledge,
You have never caught
the scent of True knowledge.
With head all warm
to rational philosophy,
The heart is cold
to mystical wisdom.
When you become fond
of knowledge of conventions,
You are low even at its heights.
The key of conventional knowledge opens no doors.
It only creates more locks.
In its meaning one finds no meaning.
In studying it, one is not enlightened.
Its indications show no way;
The news it gives gladdens no heart.

Shaikh Bahā'i

EXOTERIC KNOWLEDGE, AND KNOWLEDGE OF ITS EXTERNAL ASPECT, ESOTERIC KNOWLEDGE, AND KNOWLEDGE OF ITS INTERNAL ASPECT
('elm-e ẓāher wa 'elm-e ẓāher-e ẓāher wa 'elm-e bāṭen wa 'elm-e bāṭen-e bāṭen)

Kharaqāni said, "Knowledge may be exoteric and external, and it may be esoteric and internal. Exoteric and external knowledge is that which the learned doctors expound, while esoteric knowledge is that which the selfless communicate to one another, and knowledge of the internal aspect is the mystery that the selfless enjoy with God, being inaccessible to created beings."

TA 695

Knowledge is of two kinds: exoteric and esoteric. Exoteric is for the exegetes, those who recite Traditions, and the jurisprudents. The esoteric is for the Sufis.

MH 62

THE KNOWLEDGE OF THE INTELLECT, THAT OF SPIRITUAL STATES, AND THAT OF MYSTERIES
('elm-e 'aql wa 'elm-e aḥwāl wa 'elm-e asrār)

Ebn 'Arabi divides knowledge into three categories: that of the intellect, that of spiritual states, and that of mysteries.

He further distinguishes two kinds of knowledge of the intellect: that which is necessary and self-evident, and that which is acquired and theoretical. The latter kind is acquired through theorizing on the basis of a proof. The acquisition thereof is conditional on the nature of the given proof and others of its genre. It is characterized by the fact that the more fully it is expounded, the better its meanings are understood and the more palatable it is to the comprehending listener.

The knowledge of spiritual states can only be acquired through savour *(dhauq)*. No one dominated by reason is able to circumscribe or establish proofs to arrive at knowledge of spiritual states. The experience of this knowledge may be compared with the sweetness of honey, the bitterness of patient endurance, the pleasure of sexual intercourse, ecstasy, yearning and the like, the kinds of things that can be tasted only through direct experience.

The knowledge of mysteries is higher than the spiritual level of the intellect. It involves the imparting *(elqā')* of the Holy Spirit to the heart and is particular to prophets and friends of God *(wali),* being of two kinds:

1) A knowledge that is similar to the theoretical side of intellectual knowledge *('elm-e 'aql),* being expressed through the intellect in such a way that the intellect experiences it, yet not in a thinking or theoretical way, but rather in the form of a gift, or of a bestowal.

2) A knowledge that is itself of two kinds: a) one that is connected to the knowledge of spiritual states, though nobler than that; and b) one that is the knowledge of informing *(ekhbār),* containing both veracity and falsehood in its very essence, unless the veracity and infallibility of the informer has been established, as in the case of informing on the part of prophets, where it is understood that they are incapable of falsehood.

EA 153

KNOWLEDGE FROM GOD, WITH GOD, AND OF GOD
('elm mena'llāh wa 'elm ma'a'llāh wa 'elm be'llāh)

Moḥammad ebn Faḍhl Balkhi says that knowledge is of three kinds: from God, with God, and of God.

Knowledge of God is the knowledge of gnosis *('elm-e ma'refat),* whereby God is known to all His prophets and friends *(wali).* It is only through gnosis that they may come to know Him, because the Absolute is beyond reasons, where the devotee's rational knowledge cannot become a reason for gnosis of God, because the only reason for this can be His guidance and information.

Knowledge from God is the knowledge of the religious law *('elm-e shari'at),* which God has decreed to us and to which He has enjoined us.

Knowledge with God is the knowledge of the stations of God's Path and information about the degrees of the friends of God.

KM 18

VERBALLY COMMUNICATED, INSPIRED, AND INVISIBLE KNOWLEDGE
('elm-e khabari wa 'elm-e elhāmi wa 'elm-e ghaibi)

Verbally communicated knowledge is heard by the ear, inspired knowledge by the heart, and invisible knowledge by the soul.

Verbally communicated knowledge is external, so that it may be uttered by the tongue. Inspired knowledge arrives in the heart to be expressed. Invisible knowledge arrives in the soul to express moment. Verbally communicated knowledge is in the telling, inspired knowledge in the guiding, and invisible knowledge in the bestowing of Divine favor.

Verbally communicated knowledge is referred to in the Koranic passage: "So, know, [Moḥammad] that there is no god but God." (XLVII: 19) Inspired knowledge is referred to in the passage concerning "those who were given knowledge before [the Koran]." (XVII: 107) Invisibly infused knowledge is referred to in the passage concerning Kheḍhr, stating that God "had taught him knowledge from Our presence *(men ladonni)*. (XVIII: 65)

Beyond all these is a knowledge that man's illusory consciousness cannot attain, nor human comprehension *(fahm)* grasp. It is the knowledge of God through His Essence in terms of His Reality. In the words of the Koran: "And they cannot encompass it with knowledge." (XX: 110)

KAM VIII 399

THE KNOWLEDGE OF ALLUSION, OF LOVING-KINDNESS, OF GNOSIS, OF REALITY, AND OF DIVINE UNITY *('elm-e eshārat wa 'elm-e maḥabbat wa 'elm-e ma'refat wa 'elm-e ḥaqiqat wa 'elm-e tauḥid)*

Of the five kinds of knowledge, the knowledge of allusion washes away custom; that of loving-kindness, reason; that of gnosis, attachment to conventions of the world; that of Reality, dispersion; and that of Divine Unity, attachment to conventions of any kind [including self], where everything is washed away but God.

TSA 200

THE KNOWLEDGE OF SERVANTHOOD AND THAT OF LORDSHIP *('elm-e'obudiyat wa 'elm-e robubiyat)*

Jonaid said, "God desires that His servants have two kinds of knowledge: knowledge of the science of servanthood, and knowledge of the science of Lordship. Whatever else there is besides these is indulgence of the *nafs*."

TA 437

KNOWLEDGE OF THE ETERNAL AND OF THE TRANSITORY *('elm-e qadim wa ḥādith)*

It has been said that intentional knowledge *('elm-e qaṣdi)* is consciously designated with respect to something; whereas conventional knowledge *('elm-e ettefāqi)* comes to prevail, not specifically designated by someone, but becoming knowledge through frequency of usage. This involves either an ascription to or a presupposition about a given thing, whether subjectively or objectively, without the bringing of proofs into the process.

Intentional knowledge is of two kinds: that of the Eternal and that of the transitory.

Knowledge of the Eternal is founded on the Essence of God and can in no way be compared to any of the forms of knowledge of the transitory, which are threefold:

1) Self-evident *(badihi),* which requires no premise, such as the knowledge of one's own existence or the knowledge that the universal is greater than the particular.

2) Necessary *(ḍharuri),* the acquisition of which requires no premise, such as knowledge of the permanence of the Creator and the transitoriness of 'accidents'.

3) Rational *(estedlāli),* which is acquired without reflection or speculation. This knowledge is not ordained for the devotee.

TJ

IMITATIVE KNOWLEDGE *('elm-e taqlidi)*

Imitative knowledge is said to be that which is acquired through the imitation of others, such as the exoteric sciences, the sciences of jurisprudence, the principles of religion, the commandments of the Shari'at, philosophy, and so forth.

FLM

Imitative knowledge is only for self-advertisement; when it finds a purchaser, it glows with delight.

MM II 3265

REALISED KNOWLEDGE (*'elm-e taḥqiqi*)

Realized knowledge is acquired through realization, such as Divine knowledge, the knowledge of the friends of God and the perfected ones.

FLM

The purchaser of realized knowledge is God; its market is always splendid.

MM II 3266

THE KNOWLEDGE OF RELIGION: KNOWLEDGE OF THE RELIGIOUS LAW, THE SPIRITUAL PATH, AND DIVINE REALITY
(*'elm-e din: 'elm-e shari'at wa ṭariqat wa ḥaqiqat*)

The knowledge of religion (*'elm-e din*) falls into three categories: knowledge of the religious law (Shari'at), of the spiritual Path (*ṭariqat*), and of Divine Reality (*ḥaqiqat*). The Shari'at is to be taught, the *ṭariqat* to be acted upon, and *ḥaqiqat* to be discovered.

Concerning the Shari'at, the Koran enjoins: "Ask the followers of Remembrance (*dhekr*)..." (XVI:43 & XXI: 7)

Concerning the spiritual *ṭariqat*, it urges: "Seek the way of approach to Him..." (V: 35)

Concerning *ḥaqiqat*, it states: "And We taught him [Kheḍhr] knowledge from Our presence (*men ladonnā*)." (XVIII: 65)

God has assigned the *shari'at* to the teacher, the *ṭariqat* to the master, and *ḥaqiqat* to Himself.

KAM V 394

The knowledge of *ḥaqiqat* has three corner-stones: 1) knowledge of God's Essence and His Uniqueness (*waḥdāniyat*) and denial of similitude (*tashbih*) with respect to His Pure Essence; 2) knowledge of His Attributes and their dictates; 3) knowledge of His Acts and His wisdom in them.

Knowledge of the Shari'at has three corner-stones: 1) the Book; 2) the Custom (*sonnat*); and 3) consensus (*ejmā'*).

KM 15

When Jonaid was asked about the knowledge of Reality, he explained, "It is knowledge that is infused and Divine, any attribute of which has disappeared, such that Reality alone remains."

KAM VII 196

THE KNOWLEDGE OF DIVINE UNITY, OF GNOSIS, AND OF THE COMMANDMENTS OF THE *SHARI'AT*
('elm-e tauḥid, 'elm -e ma'refat wa 'elm-e aḥkām -e shari'at)

Knowledge is of three kinds: 1) that of Divine Unity; 2) that of gnosis of God's activity in annihilating and creating, in bringing near and distancing, in causing to die and bringing to life, in assembling and dispersing, in rewarding and punishing; and 3) knowledge of the commandments of the Shari'at.

The one who knows the first is called Divine, of the second otherworldly, and of the third worldly.

MH 56

INSTRUCTED AND INHERITED KNOWLEDGE
('elm-e derāsat wa 'elm-e werāthat)

The instructed knowledge is that which can be acted upon only if one studies and learns it, whereas one cannot experience or control inherited knowledge unless one has acted in accordance with instructed knowledge.

Hence, instructed knowledge is the introduction to practice, and inherited knowledge is the result of practice. Knowledge of truths is faith, which is handed down as a legacy to those who know. It involves a spiritual relationship of fatherhood and prophecy, where the prophets are spiritual fathers, and those who know God are their spiritual children or descendants.

Instructed knowledge is the same as exoteric knowledge, while inherited knowledge cannot be acquired without piety.

MH 65

Acquire from Him inherited knowledge;
Cultivate it for what is to come.

Shabestari

BENEFICIAL AND DETRIMENTAL KNOWLEDGE
('elm-e nāfe' wa 'elm-e ḍhārr)

The sign of beneficial knowledge is that it increases piety, humility and non-being in the *nafs,* and fans the flames of yearning and the seeking of God.

The sign of detrimental knowledge is that it increases arrogance, vainglory, conceit, and seeking after the world.

MH 59

GOD'S AND MAN'S KNOWLEDGE
('elm-e khodāwand wa 'elm-e khalq)

Man's knowledge vanishes when compared to God's, for God's knowledge is one of His Attributes, subsisting in Him Whose Attributes are infinite; whereas our knowledge is one of our own attributes of, subsisting in ourselves, whose attributes are finite. According to the Koran: "And you have been given only a little of knowledge." (XVII: 85)

KM 13

APPARENT, LATENT, AND DIVINELY INFUSED KNOWLEDGE *('elm-e jali wa 'elm-e khafi wa 'elm-e ladoni)*

According to the Koran: "And We taught him [Kheḍhr] knowledge from Our presence." (XVIII: 65)

Knowledge is that which rests on proof and removes ignorance. It has three degrees:

1) Apparent knowledge, which is manifest and acquired either through direct observation *('eyān),* through properly sought emanation, or through the correctness of long experience.

2) Latent knowledge, which grows in a cleansed inner consciousness *(serr)* through purified sowing, irrigated with the unmitigated rigor of this knowledge. It is found in the veracious breaths of those of lofty aspiration during moments free of defect, but it is for attentive ears only. This is a knowledge that makes the Absent One present, renders absent the one who witnesses, and indicates the direction of Concentration *(jam').*

3) Divinely infused knowledge, which comes from God and the sustainer of which is one's very discovery of it, the vision of which is the very perception of it, and the description of which is its very actuality. Between it and the Unseen there exists no veil.

MS

INFERENTIAL, TAUGHT, AND GOD-GIVEN KNOWLEDGE
(ʻelm-e estedlāli wa ʻelm-e taʻlimi wa ʻelm-e ladoni)

The Seventy-first Field is that of Knowledge, deriving from the Field of Detachment from Self *(tafrid)*. According to the Koran: "And none will grasp [the meaning of] them but the wise." (XXIX: 43) Knowledge has three categories:

1) Rational knowledge, which is the fruit of the intellect, the result of experience, and the domain of discrimination with which human beings have been graced in accordance with the difference in their degrees.

2) Taught knowledge, which created beings hear from God in the form of prophetic transmission, and learn from teachers in the form of instruction, and with which those who know are mighty in both worlds.

3) God-given knowledge, which consists of three forms of knowledge: that of wisdom in God's works found through signs, that of reality which one discovers through signs in communication with God, and that of wisdom emanating from God through the Unseen, this being the knowledge bestowed on Khedhr,

SM

How can each and every wing fly across the oceans?
Only God-given knowledge will carry you to the place of God.

MM III 1125

He returned, saying, "Pardon me O Mohammad,
O you to whom belong the graces of God-given knowledge."

MM I 813

God-given knowledge is that which the intimates of God come to know and understand through Divine instruction and inculcation, not through intellectual reasons or reported testimonies. This is exemplified in the case of Khedhr indicated in the Koran, "And We taught him knowledge from Our presence." (VIII: 65)

The difference between the knowledge of certitude and divinely infused knowledge is that the former involves perception of the light of the Divine Essence and Attributes, while the latter involves perception of spiritual realities and worlds directly from God. It has three categories: prophetic revelation, inspiration, and heart-discernment.

MH 76

Shedding of the conventions of knowledge through God-given knowledge occurs whenever vision of the Unseen overcomes a Substitute *(abdāl)*. When Divine recognitions become revealed in the tables of the angelic realm, he acts upon what he sees, although conventions no longer apply to him, as was the case with Khedhr. (Koran XVIII: 71-82)

The gnostic said, "Exoteric knowledge does not conflict with infused knowledge, which is simply not revealed in an external form to the exotericists."

MA 2932

THE DIFFERENCE BETWEEN INSPIRATION AND GOD-GIVEN KNOWLEDGE *(farq-e elhām wa 'elm-e ladoni)*

Ebn 'Arabi distinguishes between inspiration and God-given knowledge in the following manner:

Inspiration is knowledge through spiritual practice, being accidental and temporary, coming and going, sometimes correct, sometimes erroneous. When it is correct, it is known as the knowledge of inspiration; when erroneous, it is simply inspiration. Both kinds occur in the material world.

God-given knowledge, on the other hand, is lasting and is always correct and infallible. Furthermore, it is not necessary that it occur in the material world. It is of two kinds. The first is situated in the fundamental created nature of someone, like the knowledge of animals or infants, whether to their benefit or to their detriment. This is a form of necessary knowledge. The second kind is not situated in the created nature, but rather, arises from the result of actions, such that God favors a devotee, causing him to perform some righteous action upon the completion of which He confers a form of knowledge the like of which that person has never before been favored.

EA 168

THE OBSCURE KNOWLEDGE *('elm-e majhul)*

God has taught knowledge of the mysteries of Lordship and devotion to His chosen ones, revealing the reasons for commandments and ordained things to them. Accordingly, they come to know, in the form of knowledge, that which the clerics do not know. Then, with the ear of the elect they hear, from God, knowledge that cannot be acquired externally. This is God-given knowledge.

According to the Koran, "And We taught him (Kheḍhr) knowledge from our presence." (XVIII: 65) The Prophet said, "Indeed only those who know God know of the hidden form of knowledge."

The gnostic said, "The obscure knowledge is knowledge of the mystery of the mystery of all conventions and determinations."

MA 269

If those who are familiar with the eternal knowledge and have witnessed the pre-eternal decree did not exist in the realm of Lordship, the rest of creation would not use such terms as pole *(ostowa)*, aspect *(wajh)*, essence *('ain)*, audition *(sama')*, God's hand *(yad)* and God's foot *(rejl)*, and would not speak to the rest of humanity of special attributes and the chosen Koranic letters, A *(alef)*, L *(lām)* M *(mim)* and S *(ṣād)*. The letters of the alphabet are the source of the mysteries of the eternal Names and Attributes. They are God's instructions for the birds of the gardens of the Unseen and for the dwellers of the Divine Throne. God informs them of the mysteries of Attributes and Truths of the Essence and the changing waystations of love, the yearning of the essence of loving-kindness, of gnosis, Divine Unity, everlastingness, pre-eternity, and the mysteries of singularity in the robe of Majesty and Beauty.

All of these belong to the obscure knowledge that is exclusive to Mohammad, Adam, Abraham, Moses, Jesus, Esraphil, Gabriel, as well as to the sincere ones including the companions of the Prophet, his followers, the close friends of God, Sufi masters, the loved gnostics, and the advanced ones in Union, who fly with the wings of Attributes around the pavilions of the Grandeur and the attractions of subsistence. They are robed in the lights of loving-kindness and dressed in the eternal mysteries of the treasures of the unseen and hidden lights.

SS 59

The Station of the Revelation of the obscure knowledge of God's predetermination is a station that all created beings, believers, unbelievers and the corrupt alike, experience in the after-life. This marvel is one of the noble wonders, occurring in the course of revelation of that which lies within the inner aspect of the things that are predetermined. It involves the visionary disclosure of the mystery of the mystery and the unseen of the unseen, where one learns of eternal grace from God. This is a moment when one sees the manifestation of God's Majesty as an Eternal Attribute, shorn of any wrathful aspect and manifested to every particle. At this point, phenomenal existence and all therein becomes drowned in the light of God's Grace, the veil of the Eternal Wrath being removed from created beings; and all without exception endure forever in the light of God's Beauty and no one becomes subjected to the dictates of God's Wrath thereafter.

The gnostic said, "This is one of the special characteristics of the truths of the Unseen that have been revealed to me."

MA 305

THE DARKNESS OF IGNORANCE AND THE DARKNESS OF KNOWLEDGE *(ẓolmat-e jahl wa ẓolmat-e 'elm)*

Shāh Shojā Kermāni said, "The ignorant one lives in the darkness of his ignorance. The man of knowledge resides in the darkness of his knowledge, and this is the greater darkness.

TSS 185

KNOWLEDGE AND THE INTELLECT *('elm wa 'aql)*

Knowledge is a light from the lamp of prophecy in the heart of the believing devotee whereby he finds the way to God or to His works or to His commandments. This knowledge is especially characteristic of human beings. It is excludes sense or intellectual perceptions.

The difference between the intellect and this knowledge is that the former is an inborn light whereby righteousness is distinguished from corruption and good from evil. It is possessed by believer and infidel alike while elect knowledge is exclusive to the believer.

MH 56

GNOSIS *(ma'refat)*

In Sufi terminology, gnosis means knowing God. This knowing

can not be acquired. One either comes to know God Himself, beholding through Him, His signs and effects, or else He makes one acquainted with His effects by means of the creation, so that one may become aware of Him in terms of His effects. In either case, the Sufis understand gnosis to be related to God's guidance and direction.

***

The heart that knows light
and purity through gnosis
Sees God first in
All that it beholds.

Shabestari

Gnosis signifies the perceptions of God's epitomized knowledge in the detail of the individual forms of multiplicity. The gnosis of Lordship signifies the perception of the Divine Essence and Attributes in the individual forms of Acts, of transitory occurrences and of Divine transmissions, once one has come, through epitomized knowledge, to know that the true being and absolute agent is God.

MH 70

When Abo'l-'Abbās Sayyāri was asked about gnosis, he explained, "It is the shedding of gnosis."

TA 778

Gnosis is a world
without end,
An ocean which is boundless,
infinite.

Wisdom about the existence
of the creation is gnosis;
"I was a hidden treasure"
describes this attribute.

M 90

Abu Esḥāq Ebrāhim ebn Dā'ud al-Qaṣṣār ar-Roqqi said, "Gnosis is the affirmation of God, shorn of illusory notions. In other words, knowing God beyond the illusory *(wahm)* perspective of created being and remote from intellectual perception."

RAs 125

It has been said that when one comes to know God in terms of the Essence, one becomes speechless. When one knows Him through his Attributes, one becomes talkative, for one is still in fluctuation *(talwin).* Once one comes to enjoy gnosis of the Essence, one has attained stability *(tamkin).*"

KF 996

In the early stages, gnosis involves the knowing of God in terms of His Attributes and His qualities, while in the final stages, it means comprehending the very Essence of Reality.

RSh IV 182

Gnosis means knowing the drop in the ocean and the ocean in the drop.

RSh II 166

Ebn 'Aṭā' said that God causes the ordinary to come to know Him in terms of their created being, as referred to in the Koranic passage: "Will they not look at camels, how they are created?" (LXXXVIII: 17)

He causes the elect to come to know Him in terms of His words and Attributes, as referred to in the passages: "Will they not then ponder on the Koran?" (IV: 82); "And We reveal of the Koran that which is a healing and a mercy for believers," (XVII: 82) and "God's are the most beautiful names; invoke Him by them." (VII: 180)

He causes the prophets to come to know Him in terms of His Essence, as referred to in the passages: "And thus have We inspired in you [Moḥammad] a spirit of Our Command," (XLII: 52) and "Have you not seen how your Lord has spread the shade?" (XXV: 45)

The ordinary find a way to the Agent through His Acts, the elect to the Attributes and Names through His Attributes and Names, and the prophets to His Essence by way of His Essence.

KST 158

Jonaid said, "Gnosis means the discovery of your ignorance in the light of the God's knowledge as the basis; that is to say, you know that insofar as you are you, you are ignorant of God, and insofar as you have come to know Him, you know that the knowing is He."

KST 166

When Jonaid was asked for further comment, he said, "God is both the Gnostic and the Known; that is to say, in order for the God-knowing gnostic to arrive at knowledge of Him, He makes Himself known in such a way that the gnostic, in turn, becomes known by God."

KST 167

When Abu Sa'id Kharrāz was asked about gnosis, he explained, "Gnosis comes through two factors: 1) God's own generosity, and 2) the utmost expenditure of effort on the part of the devotee."

LT 35

Every special thing that we have mentioned is the result of gnosis which, in turn, is the result of the vision *(ro'yat)* of the Known One. This is the only gnosis that is not an expression of the subtleties of God's Acts and the light of His Names and Attributes. Such gnosis does not involve the reality of gnosis, as it is strictly concerned with the conventions of gnosis. The True gnosis is knowing the manifestation of God as He presents Himself in the form of His Essence and Attributes, by way of theophany, nearness, and direct experience of the sweetness of loving-kindness in the heart from unseen things. Consequently, one comes to know God through God, not through what is other than God.

Gnosis has both a general and a special aspect, both of which are referred to in the Koranic passage: "God is the light of the heavens and the earth," (XXIV: 35) where the light represents God's signs revealed to all, and His Essence and Attributes revealed to the few. General gnosis is expressed in statements and indications, which cannot express special gnosis because the tongue falls mute in attempting to communicate God's Reality, while the heart becomes annihilated in its failure to achieve perception of Him. Not even that most eloquent of created beings, the Prophet, was able to describe the theophany when God revealed Himself as the Known One, expressing his inability to perceive the Majesty of the Eternal, in saying, "I cannot reckon the praise for You; it is as if You are praising yourself."

Aḥmad ebn 'Aṭā' said, "Gnosis is of two kinds: that of God and that of Reality." Gnosis of God means gnosis of the Unicity *(waḥdāniyat)* with respect to whatever has been revealed of God in terms of His Names and Attributes. Gnosis of God's Reality is not possible for created being, because it is prevented by God's Impenetrability *(ṣamadiyat)* and the presence of the Lordship, as indicated in the Koranic passage: "And they can not encompass it in knowledge." (XX: 110)

The gnostic said, "Gnosis is founded on the Reality of God for the sake of God and not for anything other than Him."

MA 150

Along with other gnostics, Ebn 'Arabi terms gnosis the knowledge particular to the gnostics and those whom he calls the people of God *(ahlo'llāh [ahl-e Ḥaqq])*. He considers it to be a smooth and clear way, stressing that this kind of knowledge is immune from doubt. Its proof is too sound to be open to criticism and its possessor is secure from confoundment. It is attained through practice, clear and dependable, in contrast to the approach of thinking and theory, which is subject to error.

In Ebn 'Arabi's view, gnosis involves seven kinds of knowledge. If one succeeds in these, the perception of truths comes easily with no truth remaining hidden.The seven kinds represent gnosis of the following:

1) the Divine Names;

2) theophanies of God;

3) God's address *(kheṭāb),* as appearing in the form of prescriptions of the Shari'at;

4) the perfection and the deficiency of being;

5) one's own truths;

6) that based on imaginary revelation *(kashf-e khayāli),* involving perception of the realm of contiguous and non-contiguous imagination *(khayāl-e mottaṣel wa monfaṣel);*

7) that involving knowledge of illnesses and their cures.

EA 173

The Seventy-fifth Field is that of Gnosis, which derives from the Field of Wisdom. According to the Koran: "You see their eyes overflow with tears because of what they know of the Truth." (V: 83)

Gnosis is recognition, consisting of three categories, each comprising three degrees:

1) the recognition that Being and Unicity are one and the same;

2) recognition of the Power, the Knowledge and the Compassion;

3) recognition of beneficence, loving-kindness and nearness.

The first form of gnosis is the foundation of Islam, the second that of faith, and the third that of sincerity.

The way of advancement to the first kind is through perception of the Maker's regulatory activity in the expansion and contraction of His works. The way to the second is through perception of the Maker's wisdom in recognizing individuals in classes of like things. The way to the third is through perception of God's grace in the recognition of people's actions, forgiving transgressions; this form of gnosis being the final Field of the gnostics, the alchemy of the lovers, and the Path of the elect, the heart-adorning, joy-expanding, love-opening Path.

SM

THE GNOSIS BY ACQUAINTANCE AND GNOSIS BY DEFINITION *(ma'refat-e ta'arrof wa ma'refat-e ta'rif)*

Jonaid said that gnosis is of two kinds: that of acquaintance with God, and that of definition of God through signs.

Gnosis by Acquaintanceship with God is where God makes the devotee acquainted with Himself by involving one so much with Himself that one has nothing to do with definitions, signs, reasons, or whatever.

Gnosis by definition of signs is where God introduces Himself in such a way that the devotee comes to know Him through definitions reasons, proofs, and signs.

KST 157

RATIONAL AND VISIONARY GNOSIS *(ma'refat-e estedlāli wa ma'refat-e shohudi)*

As the Sufis express it, gnosis is a form of knowledge that admits of no doubt whenever God's Essence and Attributes become known. Gnosis of the Essence is where one knows that God is a unique *(wāhed)* and singular *(fard)* existent which is essential, objective and fundamental, that He is like nothing else, and that nothing can be compared to Him. Gnosis of the Attributes is where one knows God as the Living, the All-knowing, the All-hearing, the All-seeing, the the One who Wills, the One who Addresses, and as possessing other Attributes. Of course, as a transitory being, one cannot be said to have gnosis of God, for, basically, gnosis is a word describing a form of knowledge acquired once one has become annihilated, knowledge of God being eternal.

Rational gnosis is of the Creator through His signs. When one beholds God in the objects one sees, thus acquiring this form of gnosis, something of the Unseen is revealed, which may lead one to God by His signs, both outer and hidden. Now, if one confines one's reasoning to the outer aspect of the world without consideration of its inner aspect, not indicating both domains, one's reasoning is defective, missing the inner dimension. Indication of both the outer and the inner is performed by those of the rank of knowledge, whose knowledge is founded in Gnosis.

Visionary gnosis is necessary *(ḍharuri)*, involving demonstration of signs through signs, performed by those of the rank of the veracious and the visionaries.

KF 995

Gnosis may be attained in one of two ways:

1) through comfirming the Effecter by His Effects, going from His Acts to His Attributes and thence to His Essence, this being particular to the knowers;

2) through purifying the inner being, polishing away what is other than God from the inner consciousness *(serr)*, and adorning the spirit; this being the way of gnosis particular to the prophets, the friends of God *(wali)*, and the gnostics.

This second kind of gnosis, unveiling *(kashfi)* and visionary *(shohudi)*, except for those who are absolutely attracted *(majdhub-e moṭlaq)*, is attainable only by devotional practice in body, soul, heart, spirit, inner consciousness, and transconsciousness *(khafi,* the arcane). Once one is fully aware of the cause, one displays devotion *(erādat)* towards the Causer, so that one comes to be certain that the world was created for the purpose of a visionary gnosis attained through devotions and worship, not through the rationalization.

The rationalists walk on wooden legs;
Wooden legs are most unsteady.

SGR 7

RATIONAL GNOSIS, ARGUMENTATIVE GNOSIS, HOPE-GIVING GNOSIS, FEAR-INSPIRING GNOSIS AND GNOSIS OF DROWNING-IN-DIVINE-UNITY *(ma'refat-e estdlāli wa ma'refat-e eḥtejāji wa ma'refat-e rejā'-āmiz wa ma'refat-e bim-āmiz wa ma'refat-e gharq dar tauḥid)*

Rational gnosis is for mercenaries; argumentative or intellectual gnosis involves disappointment; hopeful gnosis for beggars; fearful gnosis for the rejected. Gnosis of Drowning-in-Divine-Unity gnosis - where does this stand? It is the True gnosis!

TSA 638

INTELLECTUAL, CUSTOMARY, SPECULATIVE AND VISIONARY GNOSIS *(ma'refat-e 'aqli wa ma'refat-e sonnati wa ma'refat-e naẓari wa ma'refat-e shohudi)*

And God revealed to David the following in the Zabur: "It behooves one who knows Me to fear My assaults, thereby increasing one's seeking of My forgiveness, and to rejoice in Me, thereby increasing remembrance *(dhekr)* of Me."[1]

Know that in this Tradition, God is speaking about the levels of gnosis, the first being fear, the second seeking of forgiveness, the third rejoicing, and the fourth remembrance. In the light of this, gnosis is of four kinds:

1) Intellectual gnosis, which is the level of those who fear and the station of ordinary created beings, pertaining to all creeds. Here ascription of partners to God is purely in the intellect and variance [of opinion] is attributive, not in the essence, while all are in agreement about the existence of a Creator.

2) Customary gnosis, which is the level of those who seek forgiveness and the station particular to the believers, whereby the opinion of one's intellect becomes purified of the adulteration of the passions and material nature, and one comes to see the Divinity of the Necessary Being. With this gnosis, one must make the focus the intellect, so that it may become assured and liberated from the plagues of the passions and theoretical contrivance.

The Prophet said, "Indeed, my heart becomes so beclouded that I ask God's forgiveness a hundred times a day."

3) Theoretical gnosis, which is the level of those who rejoice and the station of the elect. Know that those who rejoice adhere to the statement, "there is no God but God", such that after observing the injunctions and interdictions of the religious law and ridding themselves of the plagues of venial sins and lapses by resorting to the appeal for forgiveness, as indicated above, they display persistence in

1. Sacred Tradition.

properly observing the outer form and the spiritual reality of "there is no God but God", both vocally and in the heart. In this way they polish away the corrosion of material nature and the darkness of human traits from the mirror of the heart.

The Prophet said, "For everything there is a way of polishing, and the way of polishing the heart is with the remembrance of God."

Visionary gnosis, which is the level of the adherents of remembrance of God and the station particular to the elect of the elect, those who observe the call of "And remember God when you forget," is that which makes one subject to the heedlessness of figurative being.

MAM 21

GNOSIS OF THE ORDINARY, OF THE ELECT, AND OF THE MOST ELECT
(marefat-e 'āmm wa khāṣṣ wa khāṣṣ-e khāṣṣ)

Gnosis is of three kinds: that of the ordinary, that of the elect and that of the most elect.

The domain of the ordinary who enjoy gnosis is first of all that of God's Signs and Acts, which are testimonies *(shawāhed)* of His existence, and are sensed through the presence of His Acts. It is linked to three lights: those of the intellect, of the heart, and of faith. One roams about the testimonies by the light of the intellect, confirms truths of God's Power from the ledger of His signs by the light of the heart, and experiences the attributes of His Acts by the light of faith.

Gnosis of the elect involves recognizing of spiritual states that arise from the infusions *(wāred)* of ecstasy and are understood by those who are meant to comprehend them. The gnosis of this group is higher than the understanding of signs, for their domain is that of the Attributes. Their light is that of the lamp of the path of their gnosis. While the ordinary attain the domain of spiritual realities *(ma'nā)* by the lamp of signs, the elect go from God to God by the light of God, and come to know what is involved in God's special Acts thereby, such as the succession of spiritual states and the stability of stations, and constant visionary disclosure *(mokāshafa).* Indeed, if the wings of their spirits spread in flight within the core of Unity, they become burned, for that is the realm of the most elect, who may attain it solely through the gnosis of the most elect.

The gnosis of the most elect represents the rain-clouds of familiarity which bring the rain of the Uniqueness *(waḥdāniyat)* from the ocean of God's Self-subsistence at the fountainhead of annihilation. The suns and moons of the Attributes in the firmament of the Essence set when their souls arrive and rise with the dawning of the Universal Intellect in the desert of the Holy Spirit. Through love, all experience attainment. Through Divine Unity *(tauḥid)* they give up everything. The former is the disguised condition for subsistence, while the latter is the mystery of Divine Unity in annihilation.

RQR 23

THE DIFFERENCE BETWEEN KNOWLEDGE AND GNOSIS *(farq miān-e'elm wa ma'refat)*

Theologians make no distinction between knowledge and gnosis, but the Sufi masters call gnosis, knowledge that is concomitant with spiritual practice and spiritual state, knowledge thereof being the expression of one's states. The one who experences it is called a gnostic. On the other hand, knowledge that is devoid of spiritual meaning and does not involve spiritual practice is called simply knowledge and the one who experiences it is simply called a knower.

Thus, the knower is said to be someone whose knowledge is confined to verbal expression and is preserved without the preservation of spiritual meaning, while the gnostic is one whose knowledge concerns the spiritual meaning, the reality, of a thing. Hence, when the Sufis wish to condemn one of their fellows, they call him a man of learning. To the ordinary person, such a condemnation seems objectionable. The Sufi's reproach is not for one's having acquired knowledge as such, but for one's having abandoned the concomitant spiritual practice, for the knower is grounded in himself, while the gnostic is grounded in his Lord.

KM 498

Wāseṭi said, "Gnosis is where one witnesses with the senses, while knowledge is where one observes something in terms of the information that one has received from the prophets about it."

KF 996

Gnosis is fire and faith, light. Gnosis is discovery of God and faith, God's gift.

LT 41

WISDOM *(ḥekmat)*

In Sufi terminology, wisdom has two meanings:

1) Philosophical or intellectual, based on learning and reason. The Sufis reject this kind of wisdom.

Talk of the Minstrel and of wine
and seek less the secret of the world,
For no one has ever untied the knot
of this enigma with wisdom.

Ḥāfeẓ

If you desire to have less misery, then strive to rid yourself of this wisdom, the wisdom that is born of material nature and imagination, the wisdom that lacks the emanating grace of the light of the Majestic One.

The wisdom of the world brings increase of conjecture and doubt; the wisdom of religion soars above the firmament.[1]

2) Divine wisdom, in Sufi terminology, also known as gnosis of God *(ma'refato'llāh),* which comes through the emanation of grace *(faiḍh)* to the heart, not by way of acquisition.

***

Ḥāfeẓ, bring in hand a cup
from the spring of wisdom;
May the trace of ignorance vanish
from the slate of your heart.

Ḥāfeẓ

Wisdom signifies knowledge of the truths of things and of their attributes, their special characteristics, and the laws that govern them. Wisdom also signifies the relationship of causes to effects, the mysteries of the determination of the ordering of existent things and the actions produced thereby. "And whosoever is granted wisdom, he, indeed, has been given abundant good." (II: 269)

Whoever becomes
a sage of this work
Is ranked high
in Our esteem.

RSh IV 40

1. MM II 3201-203.

Wisdom is defined as one of the kinds of Divine knowledge that are particular to the spirit of each of the prophets cited in [Ebn Arabi's] *Foṣuṣ al-ḥekam (Bezels of Wisdom).* It dominates the spirit of that prophet through one of the Divine Names according to his fundamental aptitude and acquired capability.

RSh IV 321

In the early stages, wisdom involves gnosis of that which God has assigned to the devotee in the form of articles of faith and Islamic actions, as well as gnosis of the five principles of the Shari'at and the commandments of religion. In the final stages, it entails constancy in the state of subsistence after annihilation, involving the perfection of stability *(tamkin)* and immunity from fluctuation *(talwin).*

RSh IV 177

The practitioners of the Sufi Path maintain that wisdom involves gnosis of the plagues of the *nafs* and Satan, as well as ascetic discipline. They point out that wisdom in this sense is more specific than wisdom as knowledge *('elm-e ḥekmat),* of which it is considered to be a category.

KF 370

Wisdom is the definitive proof that serves to reaffirm belief, not to convince someone who is sceptical. According to the Koran: "And whosoever is granted wisdom, he indeed has been given abundant good," (II: 269), and in another passage: "Call to the Way of your Lord with wisdom and fair exhortation." (XVI: 125)

KF 370

Wisdom signifies knowing things as they are and accomplishing tasks to the best of one's ability, so that the human soul may attain the perfection that is its object, in both the formal and the spiritual domains. From this point of view, wisdom is of two kinds: speculative *(naẓari)* and practical.

SGR 466

Wisdom is knowledge that involves discussion of the truths of things as they exist, to the extent of human capacity. This knowledge is speculative, not mechanical or organic. Wisdom is also said to be the content of the practical-intellectual faculty, midway between cunning and stupidity, these being the two extremes of this faculty.

TJ

According to the Koran: "He bestows wisdom upon whom He wills, and whosoever is granted wisdom, he indeed has been given abundant good." (II: 269)

Wisdom represents the laws governing the spiritual state of every object in its particular situation. It is of three grades:

1) Where one gives every object its due, one does not exceed its limits, and one does not hasten beyond its designated time.

2) Where one witnesses *(moshāhada)* God's regard *(naẓar)* in His threats, one recognizes His justice in His decrees, and discerns His kindness in His prohibitions.

3) Where in one's reason one arrives at insight, in guidance one arrives at Reality, and in allusions one arrives at the finest degree.

MS

The Seventy-fourth Field is Wisdom, which stems from that of Life. According to the Koran: "He bestows wisdom upon whomsoever He wills." (II: 269)

Wisdom involves seeing something as it really is. Between reason and knowledge, it occupies a noble position, having been apportioned among the prophets and the friends of God *(wali)*. It is of three grades:

1) That of seeing, which involves the knowing of action as befits it, the placing of a thing in its proper place, and the knowing of a person within his or her particular framework. This is the essence of wisdom.

2) That of speaking, which involves carrying on every discourse within its scope, seeing the conclusion of every discourse in its beginning, and knowing the inner aspect of every discourse in its outer form. This is the foundation of wisdom.

3) That of living by wisdom, which involves maintaining a balance between kindness and compliment in one's dealings with others, between hope and fear in one's dealings with oneself, and between awe and intimacy in one's dealings with God. This is the fruit of wisdom.

SM

Whenever the gnostic contemplates the realm of the Acts by the light of gnosis, he comes to know the truths of certain signs. Among these he sees the faces of the brides of pre-eternal wisdom and becomes aware of the Divine decree concerning things and the special characteristics and subtleties thereof, which God has created in every particle. The Prophet was referring to this reality, when he prayed, "O Lord, show me things as they are."[1]

Then there appears to him the wisdom of the gnosis which is connected to the gnosis of spiritual practice and stations. This wisdom is linked to Divine inspiration, being acquired through theophany of the wisdom which is particular to the pre-eternal Attributes.

According to the Koran: "He bestows wisdom upon whomsoever He wills." (II: 269) The Prophet stated, "For whomsoever dedicates forty mornings to God, the wellsprings of wisdom from ages past appear on his tongue."

The gnostic said, "Wisdom is the kernel of gnosis."

MA 147

THE WISDOM ABOUT WHICH ONE KEEPS SILENT *(ḥekmat-e maskut 'anhā)*

According to the Sufis, the wisdom about which one keeps silent involves mysteries about which one can speak to no one.

KF 370

The wisdom about which one keeps silent involves the mysteries of Reality, the perception of which is beyond the awareness of the exoteric clergy and ordinary people, for they would be corrupted, or even devastated, if they were aware of them.

I cannot express
this secret in writing;
The gnostic can't even
tell it most subtly.

It is related that the Prophet was going around Medina with several of his Companions, when a frail ascetic woman came out of her place of retreat and begged him to honor her hovel by paying her a visit. The Prophet assented and went in. He saw a fire blazing there and the woman's children playing around it. "O Prophet of God!" she cried, "Is God more kind to His devotees than I am to my children?" "God is more kind," replied the Prophet, "for He is the Most Kind of the Kind!"

1. *Traditions of the Prophet,* vol. I, pp.32-33.

"O Prophet of God!" she rejoined, "I don't want to throw my children into the fire, but God does cast His devotees therein! Yet you say that He is more kind than I am!" The narrator of this incident relates that the Prophet burst into tears and exclaimed, "This is the way God has revealed it to me!"

Not every secret that you know
can be told;
Not every pearl that you find
can be strung.

RSh IV 41[1]

THE OBSCURE WISDOM *(ḥekmat-e majhul)*

The causes governing the appearance of obscure wisdom is something that is concealed from us. Examples of such things are the suffering inflicted upon some devotees, the death of children, and condemnation to everlasting hell-fire. It is incumbent upon us to accept such things, to the point of contentment if they occur to us, and to believe in the justice and right thereof.

Whatever the Wise
Arbiter decrees
Is just, for He
bestows munificence.

RSh IV 42[2]

SPOKEN WISDOM *(ḥekmat-e manṭeq behā)*

Spoken wisdom consists of the sciences of the religious law *(shari'at)* and the Path *(ṭariqat),* where the former may be known and spoken of to all, while the latter is known but only spoken of by those who follow the Path.

RSh IV 40[3]

THE ALL-EMBRACING OR ELECT WISDOM *(ḥekmat-e jāme' or ḥekmat-e khāṣṣa)*

The all-embracing or elect wisdom involves knowing and acting

1. ES 62.
2. *Ibid.*
3. ES 61.

on what is right, and knowing and avoiding what is wrong, as indicated in the Prophet's prayer: "O Lord, show what is right for what it is and bless us with adherence to it, and show us what is wrong and bless us with avoidance of it."[1] In the same light is another entreaty of the Prophet: "O Lord, show me things as they are."[2]

RSh IV 40

THE WISDOM OF ILLUMINATION *(ḥekmat-e eshrāqi)*

The wisdom of illumination is based equally on spiritual savour *(dhauq)* and rationalization *(estedlāl).* It is the school of philosophy which Shehābo'd-Din Yaḥyā Sohrawardi (d. 587/1191) founded on the basis of Avicenna's [Abu 'Ali ebn Sinā] Peripatetic philosophy (derived from Aristotle), Islamic Sufism, other Greek schools (notably Plotinus's Neoplatonism) and pre-Islamic Iranian thought (called the Pahlavi school by Sohrawardi).

***

THE WISDOM OF SPEECH, THAT OF DEEDS, AND THAT OF SIGHT *(ḥekmat-e goftār wa ḥekmat-e kerdār wa ḥekmat-e didār)*

When Shams was asked about wisdom, he replied, "Wisdom is of three kinds: that of speech, that of deeds, and that of sight."

The wisdom of speech belongs to the exoteric clergy, that of deeds to the worshippers, and that of sight to the gnostics.

The word, *ḥekmat* (wisdom), has four letters [in the Arabic alphabet: *ḥ-k-m-h],* which stand for its four roles respectively. They are: the life of hearts *(ḥayāto'l-qolub),* remover of cares *(kāshefo'l-korub),* preventer of sins *(māne'o'dh-dhonub)* and guide of hearts *(hāde'l-qolub).*

The wise one is never angry with anyone who opposes him and never harbors ill-will towards anyone who treats him harshly.

MqS 208

---

1. *Aḥādith-i Mathnawi,* B. Fruzānfār. Tehran, 1955. No. 116.
2. *Traditions of the Prophet,* vol. I, pp. 32-33

KNOWLEDGE AND WISDOM *('elm wa ḥekmat)*

Knowledge is a guide and wisdom (that is, the recognizing of the truths of beings) is the interpreter of guidance. Accordingly, knowledge is for appealing to ordinary people, while wisdom is for appealing to particular persons who are gnostics.

TKQ 263

KNOWLEDGE, GNOSIS, AND WISDOM *('elm wa ma'refat wa ḥekmat)*

The prophets are manifestations of the Wise One, and wisdom involves knowledge of the truths of things and action on the basis thereof. Accordingly, wisdom is of two categories: that of knowledge and that of action.

Knowledge involves the perception of truths through their properties, while gnosis involves the perception of truths in themselves.

On the other hand, wisdom that involves both knowledge and action is more complete and developed than either knowledge or gnosis.

NsN 24

PHILOSOPHY *(falsafa)*

Philosophy involves making oneself homogeneous with God, as much as one humbly can, for the purpose of attaining eternal bliss. As the Prophet stated: "Characterize yourselves with God's character,"[1]. Make yourself homogeneous with God in comprehending those things that are to be known and detaching yourself from corporeal things.

TJ 216

PERFECTION *(kamāl)*

In the terminology of the realized ones, perfection is the goal of the wayfarer who, journeying under the guidance of a perfect master, traverses stages, not through knowledge, but through purification, polishing, and contemplative vision *(shohud)*. Passing beyond

1. *Traditions of the Prophet,* vol. I, pp. 78-79.

the frontier of the sensible and the intelligible through the lights of theophanies of the Name, he arrives, to become annihilated in a ray of the light of theophany of the Essence of the One. Becoming subsistent in the Oneness *(aḥadiyat)* of the One who Abides, he realizes all the Divine Names and Attributes. Since God displays a different aspect at every level and in every manifestation, the perfect state is one where, after becoming the site of all manifestations, one becomes characterized by the adjuncts, properties, and qualities at all levels.

True perfection *(kamāl-e ḥaqiqi)* is where one descends from the stations of absoluteness and intoxication to that of limitation and sobriety, in order to be able to give guidance to those who seek it.

SGR 288

The ultimate perfection for the perfectly attained ones involves contemplative vision of the Absolute Beauty of the Essential Divine Unity.

SGR 268

In the ocean of Your perfection,
the perfect become imperfect;
In the essence of Your acceptance,
imperfect ones become perfect.

Sana'i

Never depart from the road
on which is the guide to the city
Of perfection, if you're an adherent
to the Path of perfection.

Nāṣer Khosrau

Perfection means the realization of Being, as opposed to material perfection. That is to say, it is a matter that is desirable from the point of view of common sense, of reason, and of the religious law. Furthermore, a perfected person is one who encompasses the truths of all things within one's essence.

MjS 982

Whenever the one who attains perfection exercises constancy in servanthood, becoming graced with the characteristics of Lordship, he does not mix the sea of Lordship with that of servanthood, though there is no gap between the two seas. While remaining at the station of servanthood in terms of loving-kindness, he goes on to that of Lordship in terms of gnosis. At this point he has reached perfection.

The gnostic said, "Perfection is the witnessing *(moshāhada)* of Lordship from the point of view of servanthood."

MA 216

ABSOLUTE PERFECTION *(kamāl-e moṭlaq)*

Absolute perfection belongs to the Divine Essence. According to the Koran: "God is Independent of all creatures." (III: 97) Human perfection embraces all the forms of the Merciful. Perfection of the Divine Essence cannot be increased, as the True Light cannot change. The sun, in perfection, is beyond increase, while the moon waxes and wanes.

The Koran has the Prophet pray, "My Lord, increase me in knowledge!" (XX: 114)

RSh III 219

THE FIRST AND SECOND PERFECTIONS *(kamāl-e awwal wa kamāl-e thāni)*

Perfection is where the human being becomes perfected in terms of either his or her essence or its attributes. The first perfection is that of a species in terms of its essence, being the most advanced of its kind. [For example, in rationality, human beings enjoys the first perfection among creatures.]

The second perfection is where the human being becomes perfected in terms of its acquired attributes, those that are secondary to its essential nature. [For example, a person may develop and perfect an attribute in becoming an engineer or a writer.]

TJ 240

PERFECTION IN TERMS OF THE ESSENCE AND IN TERMS OF THE NAMES *(kamāl-e dhāti wa kamāl-e asmā'i)*

In Sufi terminology, there are two kinds of perfection:

1) Perfection in terms of the Essence: This involves God's manifestation through Himself for His own sake without the intrusion of anything other than Him. This perfection is engendered by Absolute Self-sufficiency, which entails God's witnessing *(moshāhada)* of Himself within Himself, inclusive of all levels and conditions, both Divine and phenomenal.

Where governing laws and the adjuncts are epitomized in their universal aspect, all are subsumed within the Essence. Self-sufficiency is called Absolute in the sense that God is witnessed as being self-sufficient beyond the detailed manifestation of the world.

God has no need to possess witnessing of the world and what it contains, for His witnessing brings together all existent things for Him by the subsuming of all within Him, in His Unity. This witnessing is vision from the Unseen that partakes of the Divine Knowledge, and involves vision of the detailed aspect [of Divine knowledge] within the epitomized aspect, the vision of multiplicity within Unity.

2) Perfection in terms of the Names: This involves God's manifestation to Himself, with vision of His Essence through the extrinsic determinations *(ta'ayyon),* that is, the world and what it contains. This vision is the direct observation *('eyān)* of Being, involving vision of the epitomized within the detailed, Unity within multiplicity. This perfection involves realization and manifestation based on the existence of the world in its detailed aspect.

KF 1265

THE DIFFERENCE AMONG PERFECTION, NOBILITY, DEFICIENCY, AND BASENESS
(farq miān-e kamāl wa sharaf wa naqṣ wa kheṣṣat)

Perfection signifies the acquisition of Divine Comprehensiveness and the truths of phenomena within a human being. The more support provided by one's pleasure in the Divine Names and the truths of phenomena, the more complete is one's manifestation. The more extensive the Divine Comprehensiveness in terms of the Attributes and Names in a lover, the more perfect he or she is. The less one takes pleasure in the Divine Names, the more deficient one is and the farther one is from the rank of Divine vicegerancy.

Nobility signifies the removal of intermediate links between the caused and the Causer. The fewer the intermediate links between an object and God and the more predominant the governance of the Necessary over that of the contingent in the object's being, the nobler the object becomes. Correspondingly, the greater the number of intermediate links, the baser the given object is. Moreover, the first Intellect and the intimate angels are nobler than the Perfect Man, but the Perfect Man is more perfect than they are.

RSh IV 136[1]

THE STATION OF PERFECTING *(ekmāl)*

According to the Koran: "This day I have perfected your religion for you." (V: 3)

This term indicates the completion of bounties, both external and internal, and the arranging of the Path, Reality, and the cultivation of the substitute *(badal)*[1] at the site of stability *(tamkin)*.

The gnostic said, "The substitute dies only when he sees himself at the station of the prophets."

MA 297

1. ES 137
1. See footnote p. 104.

BIBLIOGRAPHY

Aflāki, Shamso'd-Din Aḥmad. *Manāqeb al-'ārefin.* 2 Vols., Ankara, 1959-60.

Algar, H. trans. *The Path of Gods Bondsmen from Origin to Return.* Persian Heritage Series, Caravan Books, New York: 1982.

Āmulī, Haydar. *Naṣṣ al-noṣūṣ.* Tehran-Paris: 1975.

Āmulī, Moḥammad ebn. *Nafes al funun.* Litho edition Tehran 1895.

'Ameli, Bahā'od-Din Moḥammad, (Shaikh Bahā'i). *Kolliyāt-e Shaikh Bahā'i,* Inc. *Shir wa shekar.* Ed. Gholām-Ḥosain Jawāheri. Tehran: 1978.

Anṣāri, Khwāja 'Abdo'llāh. *Majmu'a-ye rasā'el-e Khwāja 'Abdo'llāh-e Anṣāri.* Ed. M. Shirwāni. Tehran: 1973.

. *Manāzel as-sā'erin.* Incl. *'Elal-e maqāmāt.* Ed. S. Laugier de Beaurecueil. Cairo: 1962.

. *Rasā'el-e jāme'e Khwāja 'Abdo'llāh-e Anṣāri.* Ed. Waḥid Dastgerdi. Tehran: 1968.

. *Ṣad Maidān.* Incl. *Manāzel as-sā'erin.* Ed. Rawān Farhādi. Kabul: 1976.

. *Ṭabaqāt aṣ-ṣufiya.* Ed. 'Abdo'l-Ḥayy Ḥabibi. Kabul: 1968.

___ . *Zād al-'ārefin.* Ed. M. Aurang. Tehran:1974.

Arberry, A.J., trans. *The Doctrine of the Sufis.* Partial translation of Kalābādi's *Kitāb at-ta'arrof.* Cambridge University Press: 1977.

___ , trans. *The Koran Interpreted.* Oxford University Press:

1983.

___ , trans. *Muslim Saints and Mystics.* Partial translation of 'Aṭṭār's *Tadhkerat al-auliā'*. London: 1976.

'Aṭṭār Naishāburi, Farido'd-Din. *Asrār-nāma.* Ed. S. Ṣādeq Gauharin. Tehran: 1959.

___ . *Diwān-e qasā'ed wa tarji'āt wa ghazaliyāt.* Ed. Sa'id Nafisi. Tehran: 1960

___ . *Elāhi-nāma.* Ed. Helmut Ritter. Tehran: 1980.

___ . *Manṭeq aṭ-ṭair.* Ed Helmut Ritter, Tehran, 1980

___ . *Moṣibat-nāma.* Ed. Nurāni Weṣāl. Tehran: 1977.

___ . *Tadhkerat al-auliyā'*. Ed. Moḥammad Este'lāmi. Tehran, 1975.

Auhādi Marāghi, *Diwān-e Auhādi Marāghi.* Ed. S. Nafasi. Tehran: 1961.

Bābā Ṭāher 'Oriān Hamadāni. *Sharḥ-e aḥwāl wa āthār wa dobaitihā-ye Bābā Ṭāher.* Incl. *Sharḥ wa tarjoma-ye kalamāt-e qeṣār,* ascribed to *'Aino'l-Qoḍhāt Hamadāni.* Ed. Jawād Maqṣud. Tehran: 1975.

Bākharzi, Abo'l-Mofākher. *Aurād al-aḥbāb wa foṣuṣ al-ādāb.* Vols. 2. Ed. Iraj Afshār. Tehran: 1979.

Bertels, Yevgeni, Edvardovich. *Taṣawwof wa adabiyāt-e taṣawwof.* Incl. anonymous Persian Language MS, *Mer'āt-e 'oshshāq.* Russian text translated into Persian by Sirus Izadi. Tehran: 1979.

Dā'i Shirāzi, Shāh (Shāh Dā'i-ela'llāh). *Kolliyāt-e Shāh Dā'i-ye Shirāzi.* Ed. Maḥmud Dabir Siāqi. Tehran: 1961.

Dārābi, Moḥammad. *Laṭifa-ye ghaibi.* Nurbakhsh Library, Tehran, photocopy (n.d.).

Dehkhodā, 'Ali-Akbar. *Loghāt-nāma.* Compiled under supervision of Moḥammad Mo'in. Tehran: 1947-73.

Dehlawi, Amir Khosrau. *Diwān-e kāmel-e Amir Khosrau Dehlawi.* Ed. M. Darwish. Tehran: 1964.

Ebn 'Arabi, Moḥye'd-Din. *Foṣuṣ al-ḥekam.* Ed. Abo'l-A'lā 'Afifi. Beirut: 1980.

. *Fotuḥāt al-makkiya.* 4 Vols. Cairo: 1911.

Encyclopedia of Islam (New Edition). E.J.Brill, Leiden: 1986.

Encyclopedia Iranica. Ed. E. Yarshater. Routledge & Kegan Paul, London: 1985.

‘Erāqi, Fakhro'd-Din Ebrāhim. *Kolliyāt-e ‘Erāqi.* Ed. Sa‘id Nafisi. Tehran: 1959.

Resāla-ye lama‘āt wa resāla-ye eṣṭelāḥāt. Ed. Javad Nurbakhsh. Tehran: 1974.

Ernst, Carl. *Words of Ecstasy in Sufism.* Albany, N.Y, State University of New York Press: 1985.

Furuzānfar, Badī‘ol-Zamān. *Aḥādith-e Mathnawī.* Tehran: Intishārāt-i Dāneshgāh-e Tehran: 1956.

Ghazzāli, Abu Ḥāmed Mohammad. *Kimiyā-ye sa‘ādat.* Ed. by Aḥmad Ārām. Tehran: 1954.

Gauharin., Ṣādeq. *Farhang-e Loqāt-e Mathnawi Maulana,* Tehran: 1983.

Gazzāli, Aḥmad. *Resāla-ye sawāneh wa resāla-ye dau mau‘eẓa.* Ed. Dr. Javad Nurbakhsh. Tehran: 1979.

Ghurab, Maḥmūd. *Sharḥ Fuṣūṣ al-ḥikam.* Damascus: 1985.

Ḥāfeẓ Shirāzi, Shamso'd-Din Moḥammad. *Diwān.* Ed. Sayyed Abo'l-Qāsem Anjawi Shirāzi. Shiraz: 1982.

Ḥakim, So’ād, al-. *al-Mo‘jam aṣ-ṣufi.* Beirut: 1981.

Haim, S. *New Persian-English Dictionary.* 2 Vols.Tehran: 1962.

Hamadāni, ‘Aino’l-Qoḍhāt. *Tamhidāt.* Ed. ‘Afif ‘Osairān. Tehran: 1962.

Resāla-ye lawāeḥ. Ed. R. Farmanish. Tehran: 1954,

Hamadāni, Amir Seyyed Ali. *Mashāreb al-adhwāq: sharḥ-e qaṣide-ye khamriya-ye Ebn Fāreḍh Meṣri dar bayān-e sharāb-e maḥabbat.* Ed. M. Khwājawi. Tehran: 1978.

Hātef Eṣfahāni. *Diwān.* Ed. Waḥid Dastgerdi. Tehran: 1970.

Hojwiri, ‘Ali ebn ‘Othmān. *Kashf al-maḥjub.* Ed. V. A. Zhukovsky. Leningrad: 1926.

Iraqi, Fakhruddin. *Divine Flashes.* Trans. W.C. Chittick and P. L. Wilson. London: 1982.

Jāmi, Abdo’r-Raḥman. *Diwān-e kāmel-e Jāmi.* Ed. Hāshem Rāḍhi. Tehran: 1962.

___ *Haft aurang.* Ed. Mortaḍhā Gilāni. Tehran: 1978.

Lawā’eḥ. Persian text ed. and trans. into French, Yann Richard. *Les Jaillissements de Lumiere.* Paris: 1982.

___ . *Naqd-e al-noṣuṣ fi sharḥ naqsh-e al-foṣuṣ.* Ed. William Chittick. Tehran: 1976.

Nafaḥāt al-ons. Ed. Mehdi Tauḥidipur. Tehran: 1964.

Jahāngiri, Moḥsen. *Moḥye'd-Din ebn al-'Arabi.* Tehran: 1980.

Jorjāni, 'Ali ebn Moḥammad, al-. *Ketāb at-ta'rifāt.* Ed. Ebrāhim al-Abyāri. Beirut: 1985.

Jondi, Mo'ayyado'd-Din. *Nafāto'r ruḥ wa toḥfat al-fotuḥ,* Ed. M. Herawi. Tehran: 1983.

Kāshāni, 'Abdo'r-Razzāq. *Eṣṭelāḥāt aṣ-ṣufiya.* Ed. Moḥammad Kamāl Ebrāhim Ja'far. Egypt: 1984.

___ Kāshāni, A.R. *A Glossary of Sufi Technical Terms.* Trans. N. Safwat. Octagon Press, London: 1991.

Kāshāni, 'Ezzo'd-Din Maḥmud. *Meṣbāḥ al-hedāya wa meftāḥ al-kefāya.* Ed. Jalālo'd-Din Homā'i. Tehran: 1946.

Kāshāni, Faidh. *Resāla-ye Kalamāt al-maknune.* Ed. A. Ghochāni, Tehran: 1963.

Kāshefī, Fakhro'd-Dīn 'Alī ibn Ḥosain Wā'eḍh al-. *Rashaḥāt 'ayn al-ḥayāt.* 2 Vols. Tehran: 1977.

Kalābādhi, Abu Bakr Moḥammad. *at-Ta'arrof le-madhhab ahl at-taṣawwof.* Persian trans. by Moḥammad ebn 'Abde'llāh Mostamli Bokhārā'i. *Sharḥ-e Ta'arrof,* 4 Vols. Lucknow: 1912. The author has used an a Persian commentary on the text *Kholāṣa-ye Sharḥ-e Ta'arrof.* Ed. Aḥmad 'Ali Rajā'i. Tehran: 1970.

Kermāni, Khāju *Diwān-e ash'ār-e Khāju-ye Kermāni,* Ed. A. Khorasani. Tehran: 1957.

Kermāni, Moẓaffar 'Ali Shāh. *Diwān-e Moshtāqiya.* Ed. Dr. Javad Nurbakhsh. Tehran: 1968.

Khāqānī-e Shirwāni. *Dīvān-e Khāqāni-e Shirwāni.* Inteshārāt-e Aresṭu. Tehran: 1984.

Kharaqāni, Abo'l-Ḥasan. *Aḥwāl wa aqwāl-e Shaikh Abo'l-Ḥasan-e Kharaqāni.* Incl. *Montakhab-e Nuro'l-'olum.* Ed. Mojtabā Minowi. Tehran: 1980.

Khojandi, Kamāl. *Diwān-e Kamālo'd-Din Mas'ud-e Khojandi.* Ed. 'Aziz Daulatābādi. Tehran: 1958.

Khwārazmi, Kamālo'd-Din Ḥosain. *Jawāher al-asrār wa zawāher al-anwār.* Ed. Maḥmud Jawād Shirwāni. Esfahan: 1981.

Khoshnewis, Aḥmad. *Maqālāt-e shams.* Tehran: 1970.

Lāhiji, Shamso'd-Din Moḥammad, (Asiri). *Mafātiḥ al-e'jāz fi sharḥ-e Golshan-e rāz.* Ed. Kaiwān Sami'i. Tehran: 1958.

. *Diwān-e ash'ār wa rasā'el.* Ed. Barāt Zanjāni. Tehran: 1978.

Maghrebi, Moḥammad Shirin. *Diwān-e Moḥammad Shirin-e Maghrebi.* Ed. Leonard Lewisohn. London & Tehran: 1993.

Maibodi, Abo'l-Faḍhl Rashido'd-Din. *Kashf al-asrār wa 'oddat al-abrār.* 10 Vols. Ed. 'Ali-Asghar Ḥekmat. Tehran: 1978.

Mo'in, Moḥammad. *Farhang-e Fārsi.* 6 Vols.Tehran: 1981.

Moẓaffar 'Ali Shāh Kermāni: See Kermāni, Moẓaffar 'Ali Shāh.

Monawwar, Moṣammad ebn, al-. *Asrār at-tauḥid fi maqāmāt ash-Shaikh Abu Sa'id.* Ed. Dhabiḥo'llāh Ṣafā'.Tehran: 1928.

Moslem, Abo'l-Ḥosain. *Ṣaḥiḥ.* Cairo: 1929.

Nasafi, Azizo'd-Din. *Kitāb al-ensān al-kāmel.* Ed. M. Molé Tehran/Paris: 1962.

Nāṣer Khosrau Qobādiyāni. *Diwān-e Nāṣer-e Khosrau.* Incl. *Roshanā'i-nāma* and *Sa'ādat-nāma.* Ed. Mojtabā Minowi. Tehran: 1928.

Ne'mato'llāh Wali, Sayyed Nuro'd-Din, Shāh. *Kolliyāt-e Shāh Ne'mato'llāh-e Wali.* Ed. Javad Nurbakhsh. Tehran: 1978.

. *Rasā'el-e Shāh Ne'mato'llāh-e Wali.* 4 Vols. Ed. Javad Nurbakhsh. Tehran: 1978.

Neẓami, Ganjawi, Ḥakim Elyās. *Kolliyāt-e khamsa-ye Ḥakim Neẓāmi-ye Ganjawi.* Tehran: 1972.

Nicholson, A. R. trans., ed. *The Mathnawi of Jalālu'ddin Rumi,* 4th ed., 3 Vols. London, Luzac: 1977.

___ , trans. *Kashf al-Maḥjub of Al-Hujwiri.* E. J. W. Gibb Memorial Series, Vol. XVII. London: 1911; reprint: 1976.

___ . *Selected Poems From the Dīvāni Shamsi Tabrīz.* Cambridge University Press: 1977.

Nurbakhsh, Dr. Javad. *In the Tavern of Ruin.* KNP, New York, 1978.

___ . *Traditions of the Prophet (Aḥādith).* 2 Vols. trans. L. Lewisohn and T. Graham. KNP, New York: 1981 & 1983.

___ . *In the Paradise of the Sufis.* KNP, New York: 1979.

___ . *Farhang-e Nurbakhsh.* 10 Vols. KNP, London: 1984-88. *Sufi Symbolism.* Trans. L. Lewisohn and T. Graham. 7 Vols. KNP, London: 1984-93.

___ . *Spiritual Poverty in Sufism.* Trans. L. Lewisohn. KNP, London: 1984.

. *Sufism II.* Trans. W.C. Chittick. KNP, New York: 1982.

. *Sufism V.* Trans. T. Graham. KNP, London: 1991.

___ . *Psychology of Sufism.* Trans T Graham KNP London 1992.
Olfati Tabrizi, Sharafo'd-Din Ḥosain. *Rashf al-alḥāẓ fi kashf al-alfāẓ.* Ed. Māyel Herawi. Tehran: 1983.
Penrice, John. *A Dictionary and Glossary of the Koran.* Curzon, London: 1873, rpt. 1971.
Pickthall, Marmaduke, trans. *The Glorious Koran.* London: 1930; rpt. 1969.
Qoshairi, Abo'l-Qāsem. *Tarjoma-ye resāla-ye Qoshairi.* Ed. Badi'o'z-Zamān Foruzānfar. Tehran: 1982.
___ . *ar-Resālat al-Qoshairiya.* 2 Vols. Cairo: 1912.
. *Principles of Sufism.* Trans. B. R. Von Schlegell. Mizan Press, Berkeley: 1990.
Rāzi, Najmo'd-Din, Dāya. *Merṣād al-'ebād men al-mabda' ela'l-ma'ād.* Ed. Moḥammad Amin Riyāḥi. Tehran: 1973.
. *Marmuzāt-e Asadi.* Ed Shafihi Kadkani. Tehran 1973.
Rumi, Jalālo'd-Din. *Kolliyāt-e Shams yā Diwān-e kabir.* 10 Vols. Ed. Badi'o'z-Zamān Foruzānfar. Tehran: 1959.
___ . *Mathnawi-ye ma'nawi.* Ed. R.A. Nicholson. Tehran: 1977.
Rūzbihān Baqlī Shīrāzī.*Mashrab al-arwāḥ.* Ed. Nazif M. Hoca. İstanbul Üniversitesi Edebiyat Fakültesi Yayinları, No. 1876. Istanbul: Edebiyat Fakültesi Matbaası: 1974.
. *Resālat al-qods*, incl. *Ghalaṭāt as-sālekin.* Ed. Javad Nurbakhsh. Tehran: 1981.
Sharḥ-e shaṭḥiyāt. Ed. Henry Corbin. Bibliothèque Iranienne, 12. Tehran: 1966, rpt. 1981.
Sabzawāri, Hādi, Ḥājji Mollā, (Asrār). *Diwān-e Ḥājji Mollā Hādi-ye Sabzawāri.* Ed. Sayyed Moḥammad Reḍhā Dā'i-Jawād. Esfahan: undated.
Sharḥ-e ghorar alfarā'iḍ or *Manẓuma-ye Ḥikma.* T. Izutsu and M. Mohagheg, Tehran: 1977t
Sa'di, Moṣleḥo'd-Din. *Bustān.* Ed. Nuro'd-Din Irānparast. Tehran: 1977.
. *Golestān.* Ed. Khalil Khaṭib Rahbar. Tehran: 1969.
. *Kolliyāt-e Sa'di.* Ed., Moḥammad 'Ali Forughi. Tehran: 1978.
Sanā'i, Abo'l-Majd Majdud. *Ḥadiqat al-ḥaqiqat wa shari'at aṭ-ṭariqat.* Ed. Modarres Raḍhawi. Tehran: 1976.
___ . *Diwān-e Sanā'i-ye Ghaznawi.* Ed. Modarres Raḍhawi.

Tehran: 1975.

. *Mathnawihā*. Ed., Modarres Raḏhawi. Tehran.

Ṣarrāj Ṭusi, Abu Naṣr. *Ketāb al-loma' fe't-taṣawwof.* E.J.W. Gibb Memorial Series, No. 22. London: 1914.

Schimmel, Annemarie. *Mystical Dimensions of Islam.* The University of North Carolina Press, Chapel Hill: 1978.

Shāh Ne'mato'llāh Wali: See Ne'mato'llāh Wali, Sayyed Nuro'd-Din.

Shabestari, Maḥmud. *Golshan-e rāz.* Ed. Javad Nurbakhsh. Tehran: 1976.

___ . *Majm'a-i āthār-i Shaykh Maḥmūd Shabistarī.* Tehran: Kitābkhāna-ye Ṭahūrī: 1987.

Shaikh Bahā'i See 'Āmeli, Bahā'od-Din Moḥammad.

Shirāzi, Rokno'd-Din ebn 'Abdo'llāh, Bābā Roknā. *Noṣuṣ al-khoṣuṣ fi tarjomat al-foṣuṣ.* Tehran: 1980.

Shirazi, Moḥammad Ma'ṣum.*Tarā'eq al haqā'eq.* Ed. Moḥammad Jafar Maḥjub. Tehran: 1951.

Soyuṭi, Abu Abdor-Rahmān. *Kanz-e al madfun*. Egypt: 1978.

Solami, Abu 'Abdo'r-Raḥmān. *Ketāb ṭabaqāt aṣ-ṣufiya.* Ed. Johannes Peterson. Leiden: 1960.

Steingass, F. *Persian-English Dictionary.* Tehran, 1978.

Suhrawardi, *"Ketāb Ḥekmat al-Eshrāq."* Oeuvres Philosophiques et Mystiques. Ed. Henry Corbin. 2 Vols. Académie Impériale Iranienne de Philosophie/Librairie Adrien-Maisonneuve, Tehran/ Paris: 1977.

Sohrawardi, 'Omar al-. *'Awārif al-ma'ārif.* 2 ed. Beirut: 1983.

Ṭabasi, Darwish Moḥammad. *Āthār-e Darwish Moḥammad-e Ṭabasi.* Ed. Iraj Afshār and Moḥammad Taqi Dāneshpazhuh. Tehran: 1972.

Tabrīzī, Homām. *Diwān-i Homām Tabrīzī.* Tehran: 1970.

Tabrizi, Sā'eb. *Kolliyāt-e Ṣā'eb Tabrizi,* Ed. A. Firuzkuhi, Tehran 1954.

Tahānawi, Moḥammad A'lā ebn 'Ali. *Kashshāf esṭelāḥāt al-fonun.* Ed. Asiatic Society of Bengal. Calcutta: 1982.

Wehr, Hans. *A Dictionary of Modern Written Arabic.* Rpt. Librairie du Liban, Wiesbaden: 1974.

Wensinck, A. J. *Concordance et Indices de la Tradition Musulmane.* 6 Vols. Brill, Leiden: 1936.

INDEX OF PERSIAN AND ARABIC TERMS

GENERAL INDEX

125.
'elm-e din, knowledge of religion; 133.
'elm-e ettefāqi, conventional knowledge; 132.
'elm-e ḥekmat, wisdom as knowledge; 150.
'elm-e ḥoṣuli, acquired knowledge; 121.
'elm-e ladoni; 92, 131, 133.
'elm-e ma'refat, knowledge of gnosis; 130.
'elm-e morāqabat, knowledge of watchfulness; 128.
'elm-e manqul; 120.
'elm-e qaṣdi, intentional knowledge; 132.
'elm-e shari'at, knowledge of the religious law; 130.
'elm-e soluk, knowledge of conduct on the Path; 127.
'elm-e taṣawwof, knowledge of Sufism; 125.
'elm-e tafsir wa ta'wil, exegesis and hermeneutics; 125.
elqā', imparting; 70, 98, 130.
eltebās, disguise; 51.
enbesāṭ, exhilaration; 110.
enferād, Detachment from Self; 106.
ensān-e kāmel, Perfect Man; 61, 93, 98, 100, 158.
erādat, devotion; 20, 145.
eshārat, allusion; 42.
esm-e a'ẓam, Greatest Name; 89.
'eshq, love; 52.
Esrafil; 138.
estedlāli, Rational; 132.
esteqāmat, Constancy; 32.
Eve; 60, 77, 96.
'eyān, directly observable; 123, 124, 135, 158.
faḍhl, grace; 96.
fahm, comprehension; 59, 131.
faiḍh, grace; 54, 57, 75, 86, 95, 111, 149.
faiḍh-e rabbāni, Divine emanating grace; 74.
fard, singular; 144.
fardāniyat, Singularity; 60, 90.
feṭnat, sagacity; 57.
fekr, reflection; 29, 51, 63, 79, 101.
ferāsat, heart-discernment; 36, 37, 40, 43, 59.
fo'ād, site of heart-vision; 86, 92, 97.
Foṣuṣ al-ḥekam; 150.
Gabriel; 12, 50, 52, 60, 98, 99, 100, 138.
ghairat, protectivenes; 42.
ḥabbato'l-qalb, grain of the heart; 92.
hāde'l-qolub, guide of hearts; 155.
hājes, worldly motivations; 106.
Ḥāfeẓ, Moḥammad Shamso'd-Din (d. 1389); 3, 15, 17, 18, 20, 27, 30, 34, 49, 65, 67, 149.
Ḥallāj, Manṣur (d. 922); 104.
ḥaqiqat; 133.
ḥaqiqat-e moḥammadiya; 98.
ḥayāto'l-qolub, life of heart; 154.
ḥejāb, veiling; 104.
ḥekmat- e khalqiya, material wisdom; 127.
ḥesbat, accounting; 24.

68, 70, 72, 73, 74, 75, 78, 80, 81, 82, 83, 84, 85, 87, 90, 91, 93, 94, 97, 98, 101, 103, 104, 106, 112, 115, 116, 124, 126, 128, 132, 134, 150.
nafs-e ḥaiwāni, animal soul; 85, 86.
nafs-e ammāra, commanding soul; 70, 71, 72, 74, 75, 78, 80.
nafs-e ellahi, Divine Soul; 79.
nafs-e koll; Universal Soul; 60, 61, 78, 79, 86, 95.
nafs-e lawwāma; blaming soul; 72, 74, 80.
nafs-e makara; deceiving soul; 71.
nafs-e malakiya; angelic soul; 79.
nafs-e moṭma'enna; 73, 74, 80.
nafs-e molhama, inspired soul; 74.
nafs-e monṭabe'a, ingrained soul; 76.
nafs-e nāṭeqa, rational soul; 15, 47, 68, 75, 85, 86, 89, 94, 101.
nafs-e sahhāreh, bewitching soul; 72.
nafs-e shahwāniya, sensual soul; 75.
nafs-e wāḥediya, single soul; 97.
namāz, daily prayers; 82.
Nasser Khossrau; 156.
Neoplatonism; 154.
nofus- e monṭabe, en-natured souls; 89.
Nojaid, Abu 'Amr (d. 907); 31.
noqabā', Chieftains; 104.
nun; 62.
Nuri, Abo'l Hasan (d. 907); 22, 26, 50.
'obudiyat, servanthood; 103.
oluhiyat, Godhead; 33, 92.
ommo'l-ketāb, Mother Book; 60, 61, 62.
ostowa, pole; 138.
Pahlavi school; 154.
Pedestal; 40.
Peripatetic philosophy; 154.
Pharaoh; 50, 103.
Plotinus; 154.
Primal Source; 4.
Prophet, Moḥammad; 2, 4, 9, 12, 16, 18, 19, 20, 26, 31, 32, 36, 37, 40, 49, 50, 51, 59, 62, 77, 78, 80, 82, 83, 84, 95, 96, 98, 100, 101, 102, 103, 104, 105, 107, 108, 122, 123, 126, 131, 136, 138, 141, 142, 146, 147, 152, 154, 155, 157.
qalam, pen; 49, 60, 62, 94, 96, 97.
qalam-e a'lā, Sublime Pen; 86.
qalandar; 65.
qalb, heart; 91.
qalbo'l- 'ālam, World-Heart; 98.
qalbo'l-wojud, Heart of Being; 98.
qoṭb, Pole; 50.
qowwa-ye 'āqeliya-ye naẓariya, faculty of intellectual speculation; 41
qowwa-ye motakhayyala, faculty of imagination; 11.
qowwa-ye qodosiya, faculty of sanctification ; 41.
rabb; 109.
rawān, psyche; 93.
rejh, foot; 138.
resālat, mission; 25, 119.
ro'yat, vision; 84, 92, 103, 110,

ṭariqat; 133, 153.
taṣawwor, conceptualization; 1.
tasbiḥ, glorification; 26.
taṣdiq, attestation; 15.
tashbih, similitude; 133.
tauḥid, Divine Unity; 16, 19, 32, 33, 38, 60, 82, 96, 104, 131, 134, 138, 148.
ta'wil, hermeneutics; 125.
Termedhi, Moḥammad ebn (d. ca. 908-932); 34.
Thaqafi, Abu 'Ali; 117.
Throne, Divine Throne; 40, 60, 91, 98, 138.
Tostari, Sahl ebn 'Abdo'llāh (d. 896); 103, 128.
Tradition; 2, 9, 16, 26, 36, 37, 40, 49, 51, 62, 77, 78, 83, 84, 86, 96, 93, 95, 102, 104, 105, 107, 117, 119, 122, 126, 129, 138, 142, 146, 147, 152, 154, 155.
Turk; 69.
waḥdāniyat, Uniqueness; 38, 41, 59, 90, 133, 142, 143, 148.
wāhed, unique; 144.
wāḥediyat, Unicity; 76, 90.
wahm, apprehensive faculty; 53, 101, 125, 140, 141.
waḥy-ye elāhi, Divine revelation; 101.
wājeb al- wojud, Necessary Being; 52, 59, 61, 93, 146.
wajh, aspect; 138.
walah, distracted; 2.
wali, friend of God; 56, 74, 101, 125, 130, 145, 151.
waqt; 124.
wāred, infusions; 111, 147.
Wāseṭi, Abu Bakr (d. 942); 21, 23, 37, 149.
waswasa, Satanic temptations; 106.
wesal; 2.
wojud-e ḥaqiqi, True Being; 7, 9.
yad, hand; 138.
yāquto'l-ḥamrā', Ruby; 60.
Yusof ebn Ḥosain; 104.
Zabur; 146.
ẓālem, oppressive; 74.
ẓann, opinion; 53.
zonnār, cincture; 83.